I0820071
BRUSSEL
ALOST
LOWEN
Tirlemont
St Trond
Tongres
LÜTTICH
VERVIERS
NAMUR
Huy
Malmedy
Roeselare
Ypern
TOURCOING
ROUBAIX
LILLE
TOURNAI
Renaix
Lessines
Ath
Nivelles
Gembloux
Andenne
Wavre
Hal
Grammont
Audenarde
LXXXII
15
Armentières
LENS
DOUAI
ARRAS
VALENCIENNES
Denain
MONS
CHARLEROI
Châtelet
Thuin
Maubeuge
Philippeville
Dinant
Ciney
Givet
Rochefort
Marche
St Hubert
CAMBRAI
Caudry
Le Cateau
Avesnes
Fourmies
Hirson
Bohain
ST QUENTIN
Guise
Vervins
Péronne
Albert
VII.
Charleville
Mézières
Sedan
Bouillon
Neufchâteau
LUXEMBURG
Laon
Tr. Üb. Pl. Sissonnes
1/Gren. Btl.
Chauny
Noyon
Montdidier
Compiègne
Soissons
Rethel
Vouziers
Stenay
Montmédy
Longuyon
Diedenhofen
REIMS
Fismes
Tr. Üb. Pl. Suippes
Art. Schule
Tr. Üb. Pl. Mourmelon
Epernay
CHÂLONS-S. M.
Ste Menehould
Verdun
Varennes en Argonne
Clermont en Argonne
METZ
Pont-à-Mousson
St Mihiel
Commercy
Bar-le-Duc
Toul
NANCY
1.
Vitry le François
Tr. Üb. Pl. Mailly-le Camp
Pz. Tr. Schule
St Dizier
Joinville
Château Thierry
Meaux
Coulommiers
Sézanne
Provins
Melun
Romilly s. S.
Nogent s. S.
TROYES
Sens
Brienne-le Château
Bar s. A.
Bar s. S.
Chaumont
Neufchâteau
Mirecourt
Vittel-Auzainvilliers
Montargis
Jenny
St Florentin
Forêt d'Othe
Nogent-en-Bass.
Bourbonne les Bains

VICTORY IN EUROPE

FROM D-DAY TO THE DESTRUCTION OF THE THIRD REICH

1944–1945

IN PARTNERSHIP WITH
IWM

JULIAN THOMPSON

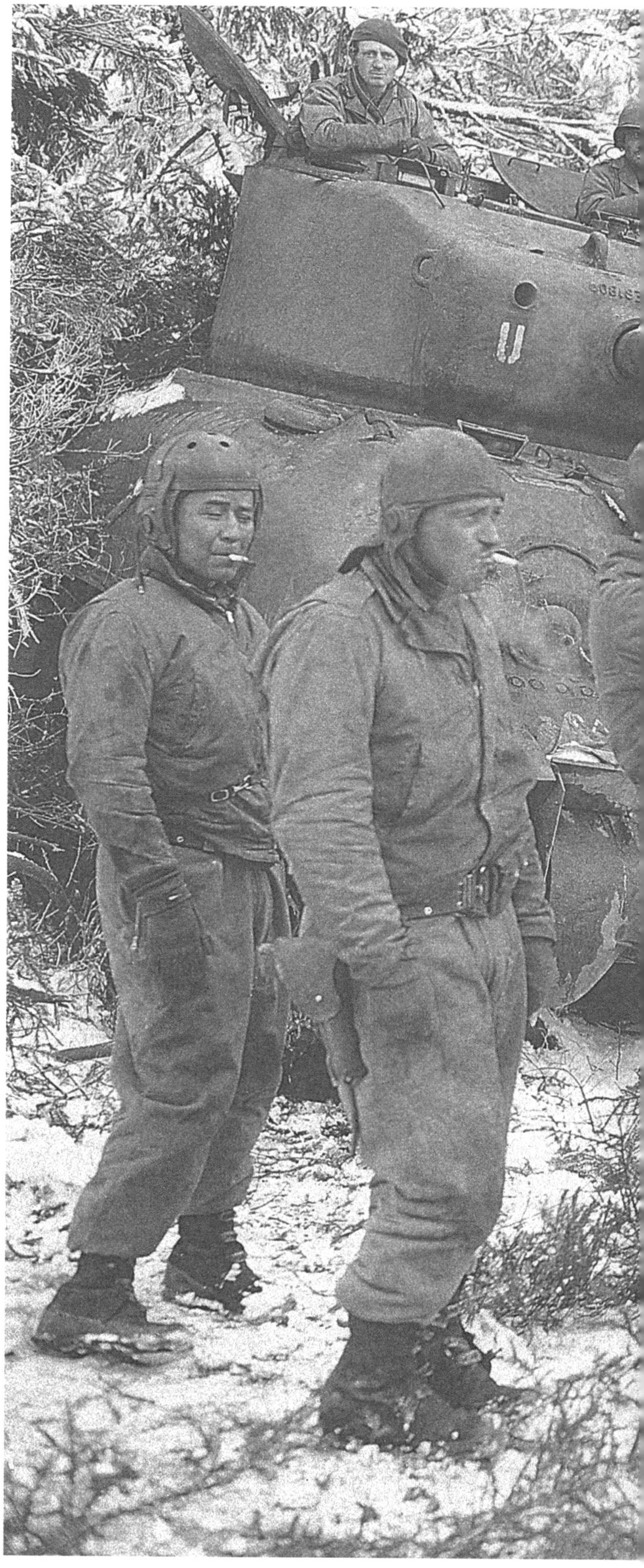

RIGHT Troopers of the US 3rd Armored Division in the vicinity of Hoton on the northern shoulder of the Bulge, awaiting orders to advance down the Liege-Bastogne Road.

Editorial research and checking: Jack Livesey
Design: Mary Ferdinand and Martin Brown

This edition published in 2025 by Welbeck
An Imprint of HEADLINE PUBLISHING GROUP LIMITED

Originally published by Carlton Books in 2005 under the title World War 2 Victory in Europe Experience.

1

Cataloguing in Publication Data is available from the British Library

ISBN 9781035425174

Printed in Dubai

HEADLINE PUBLISHING GROUP LIMITED
An Hachette UK Company
Carmelite House
50 Victoria Embankment
London EC4Y 0DZ

The authorised representative in the EEA is Hachette Ireland,
8 Castlecourt Centre, Dublin 15, D15 XTP3,
Ireland (email: info@hbgi.ie)

www.headline.co.uk
www.hachette.co.uk

CONTENTS

TeL
53
44

INTRODUCTION

VE-DAY IS A LANDMARK IN HISTORY

The 11 months between the landings in Normandy and VE-Day saw some of the toughest fighting endured by the Western Allies in the Second World War, indeed in both World Wars. This book looks at the whole north-west European campaign right up to the surrenders in May 1945. As it reached its climax with the Western Allies penetrating the Reich, the scenes which greeted the soldiers liberating the concentration camps could have left none of them in any doubt as to why they were fighting, and the rightness of the Allied cause.

The balance of the Allied forces, fighting what their overall commander, General Eisenhower, described as a "great crusade", changed considerably during the course of the fighting. It is a common misconception that for the British the fighting in the Second World War was nothing like as costly as in the First. In fact, it was safer to be on the Somme in 1916, than in Normandy in 1944. After five years of war, these casualties weighed heavily on the British manpower base.

For the Americans, the campaign in north-west Europe was the moment in which their armies blossomed into their full power. Until then it was possible to view the British as equal partners on land. From Normandy onwards this was no longer the case. By the end in Europe, the Americans fielded five armies to the British one.

The Canadian contribution to D-Day included the 21,500 men of the Canadian 3rd Infantry Division landed on Juno Beach, bombarding and escorting warships, and about half the squadrons assigned to 83 Group, Second Tactical Air Force. By war's end, the First Canadian Army had committed to the fray every volunteer for overseas duty the dominion could muster.

The campaign also saw the emergence of another army, the French. Two troops of Number 10 Inter-Allied Commando, about 120 men, commanded by Captain Philippe Kieffer landed with the 1st Special Service Brigade in Normandy. By August 1944, the numbers of Frenchmen in uniform fighting for their country's liberation had been swelled to over 260,000 by General Leclerc's 2nd Armoured Division, and General de Lattre de Tassigny's Army B (later First French Army).

The Allied air forces and navies played an indispensable part, often unseen and far away from the actual land fighting, in supporting the armies. Logistics – that unglamorous activity, so often ignored by historians – was absolutely crucial for success. At one stage, the campaign nearly foundered because supplying the fighting tip was accorded a low priority in the higher commanders' plans. Insufficient attention was given to the problem of moving supplies, especially petrol forward of the beaches, and to the early opening of the port of Antwerp after its capture.

Allied forces elsewhere contributed mightily to the success of the campaign. The landings in Normandy and subsequent campaign would not have been possible without the support of the Red Army. From 1941 to May 1945, the Soviet Union engaged the major part of the German Army in one of the bloodiest battles in history. On 6 June over 200 German divisions were deployed on the Eastern Front, leaving some sixty to face the Allies in the west. The Soviet Union lost over 11 million dead and missing in battle and 6 million prisoners.

Allied armies fighting in Italy pinned down 23 German divisions in Italy, keeping them from reinforcing Normandy.

I hope that the memorabilia, especially, will bring home to readers that however much the generals plan, without the rifleman, gunner, tank crew or truck diver, the most brilliant schemes are worthless. In the end, it is ordinary people, doing extraordinary things that win the day. The consequences of those extraordinary deeds are still with us today, and we should never forget the debt we owe.

OPPOSITE Soldiers of 15th Scottish Division with armour and half-tracks waiting for engineers to bridge a mine crater before advancing to the River Elbe.

INDEX OF MAPS

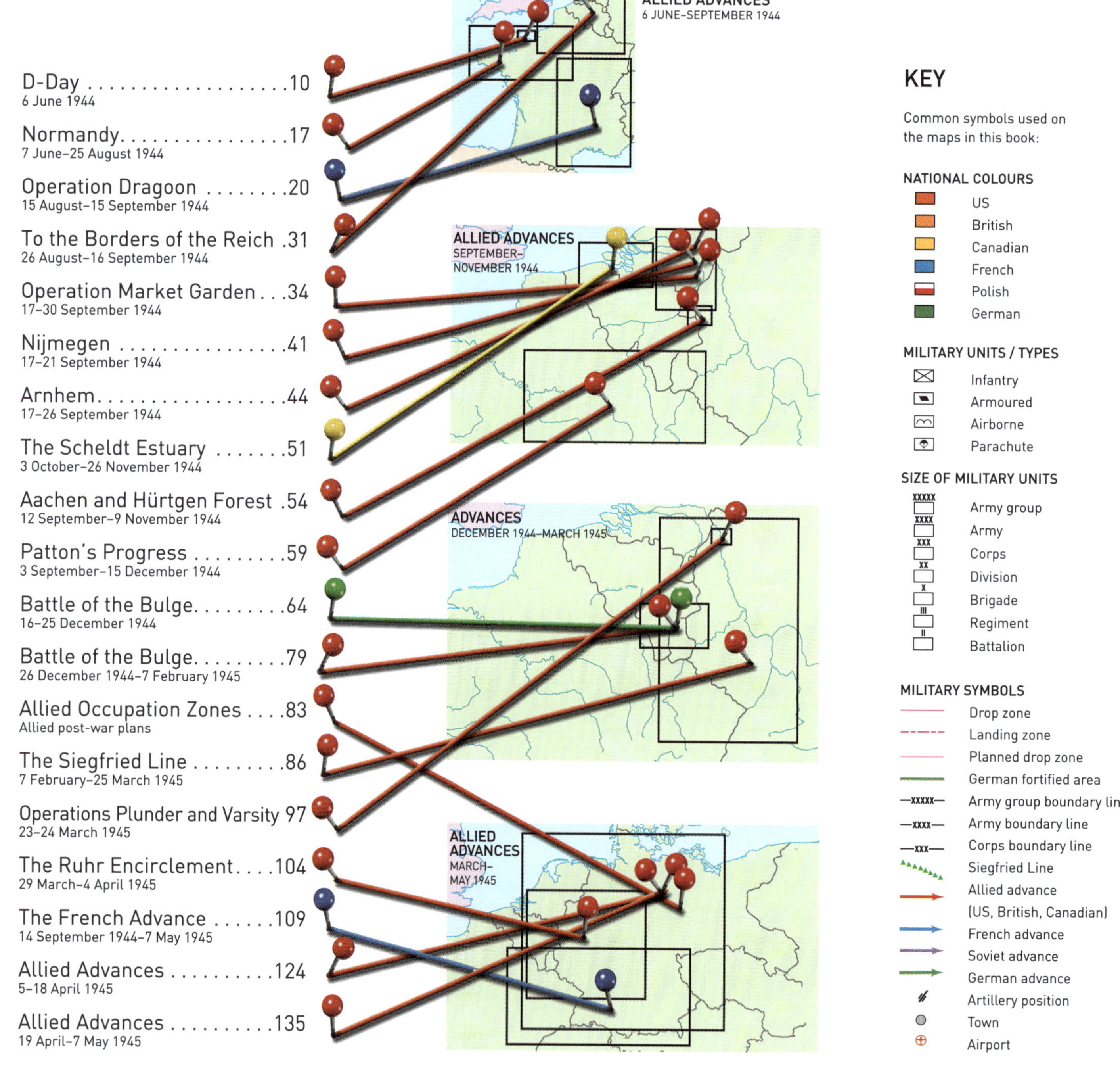

KEY

Common symbols used on the maps in this book:

NATIONAL COLOURS
- US
- British
- Canadian
- French
- Polish
- German

MILITARY UNITS / TYPES
- Infantry
- Armoured
- Airborne
- Parachute

SIZE OF MILITARY UNITS
- XXXXX Army group
- XXXX Army
- XXX Corps
- XX Division
- X Brigade
- III Regiment
- II Battalion

MILITARY SYMBOLS
- Drop zone
- Landing zone
- Planned drop zone
- German fortified area
- —xxxxx— Army group boundary line
- —xxxx— Army boundary line
- —xxx— Corps boundary line
- Siegfried Line
- Allied advance (US, British, Canadian)
- French advance
- Soviet advance
- German advance
- Artillery position
- Town
- Airport

NORTH-WEST EUROPE

Allied Advances 6 June 1944–7 May 1945

D-DAY

TUESDAY 6 JUNE 1944

ABOVE 21st Army Group badge.

The landings in Normandy on 6 June 1944 were a stupendous success. At the time some senior Allied commanders were not so confident of the outcome. General Dwight D. Eisenhower, the Allied Supreme Commander, wrote a letter accepting all the blame to be published in the event of failure. Because of bad weather the landings had been postponed by 24 hours, but, based on the forecast that the gale would blow itself out, Eisenhower eventually made the courageous decision to go ahead. The weather worked in the Allies' favour because many of the senior German commanders were absent from their headquarters – including Field Marshal Erwin Rommel, commander of the invasion beaches, who was visiting his wife in Germany. Lacking an accurate weather forecast, they

D-DAY BEACH LANDINGS

UTAH BEACH
Planned H-Hour: 06.30
Assaulting Division: US 4th Inf
Men Landed: 23,250
Casualties: c.200

OMAHA BEACH
Planned H-Hour: 06.30
Assaulting Division: US 1st Inf with elements attached from US 29th Inf
Men Landed: 34,250
Casualties: c.2,000

GOLD BEACH
Planned H-Hour: 07.25
Assaulting Division: British 50th Division
Men Landed: 24,970
Casualties: c.1,000

JUNO BEACH
Planned H-Hour: 07.45
Assaulting Division: Canadian 3rd Division
Men Landed: 21,500
Casualties: c.1,000

SWORD BEACH
Planned H-Hour: 07.25
Assaulting Division: British 3rd Division
Men Landed: 28,845
Casualties: c.630

ABOVE General Eisenhower talks to Lieutenant Strabel of the 502nd Parachute Infantry Regiment, 101st Airborne Division (the "Screaming Eagles") at Greenham Common airfield on 5 June 1944, just before the division emplanes.

"IKE" *aged 54 on D-Day, had a meteoric rise from obscurity, never having experienced war before being appointed to command the Allied force for the invasion of North Africa in 1942 and subsequently Sicily in 1943. He was selected by Roosevelt, to which Churchill begrudgingly agreed, to command the invasion of north-west Europe. His genius lay in his ability to keep a team of strong-willed naval, air and ground commanders working together towards the common goal of victory.*

ABOVE Pathfinders of British 6th Airborne Division synchronizing their watches before boarding an Albemarle at RAF Harwell. Left to right are Lieutenants Robert de Latour, Donald Wells, John Vischer and Captain Robert Mahood.

ABOVE Le Régiment de la Chaudiere, follow-up battalion of 8th Brigade, 3rd Canadian Division, landing on Juno Beach in Landing Craft Assaults (LCAs).

"MONTY" *was a highly professional and single-minded soldier who had served throughout the First World War, and who had made his reputation in the Western Desert, Sicily and Italy in the Second. He was a perfectionist, conscious that by 1944, after five years of war, Britain's limited manpower had to be husbanded carefully. Contemptuous of those lacking his experience and skilled approach to command in war, his outspokenness made him an uncomfortable partner and subordinate in a coalition.*

believed that the conditions were too rough for an amphibious or airborne operation.

Soon after midnight on 6 June 1944, the British 6th Airborne Division landed by parachute and gliders east of the River Orne and Caen Canal, and the US 82nd and 101st Airborne Divisions landed north and north-west of Carentan, on the Cotentin Peninsula. Their tasks were to protect the flanks of the beachhead, silence German batteries and seize key bridges and routes.

Soon after dawn the seaborne assault began, preceded by a massive sea and air bombardment. In the west, Lieutenant General Omar Bradley's US First Army landed on Omaha and Utah Beaches, while in the east and centre, Lieutenant General Miles Dempsey's British and Canadian Second Army landed on Sword, Juno and Gold Beaches. Of the 156,000 troops landed by sea and air, some 84,000 were British and Canadian. Nearly 80 per cent of the naval support was British and Canadian, as was half the huge air armada.

The German reaction had been slow and unco-ordinated, thanks to conflicting information and orders. The airborne landings, although badly scattered, served to conceal where the main Allied effort was to be made. Small parties of Allied airborne soldiers fought lonely battles, sometimes miles from the bridgehead, and tied down German troops that otherwise might have taken part in attacks on the seaborne troops. The seizure of the Orne and Caen Canal bridges forced the Germans to divert troops via Caen, a six-hour detour. The delays imposed on the 21st Panzer Division to switch their main effort from east of the river and canal, enabled the British to repulse counter-attacks by the only armoured formation encountered by the Allies on D-Day, and potentially the most formidable division in the lodgement area.

By nightfall, the Allies had gained a foothold in France. Surprise had been achieved; the troops had fought courageously and skilfully. Not all the D-Day objectives had been achieved, though. The outcome on Omaha Beach hung in the balance for much of the day. Only the bravery of the two American assaulting divisions, the 1st ("Big Red One") and the 29th, supported by destroyers closing on the coast and firing point-blank at the guns pinning down troops on the beach, carried the day. There were gaps between the British-Canadian and the American beaches, and a dangerous salient at Douvres between the Canadians and British I Corps. But the Allies under General Montgomery were ashore, and ready to start the Battle of Normandy.

ABOVE Follow-up wave of infantry wading ashore from a Landing Craft Vehicle Personnel (LCVP) at Omaha Beach.

6 JUNE 1944

D-DAY

KEY

Allied front line at the end of D-Day

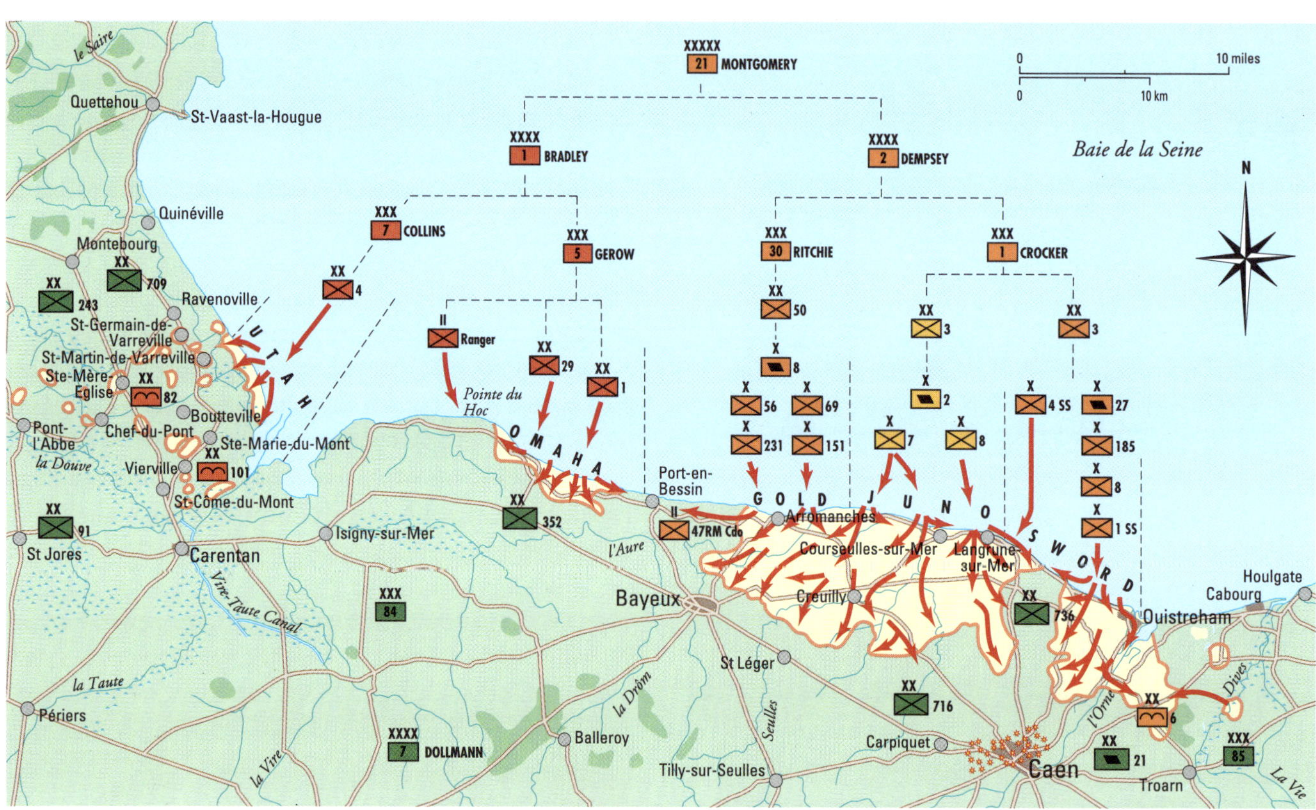

BELOW Eisenhower's handwritten note, wrongly dated, taking full personal responsibility for the D-Day landings. This was to have been published if they had failed.

Our landings in the Cherbourg – Havre area have failed to gain a satisfactory foothold and I have withdrawn the troops. My decision to attack at this time and place was based upon the best information available. The troops, the air and the Navy did all that Bravery and devotion to duty could do. If any blame or fault attaches to the attempt it is mine alone.

July 5

BELOW AND OPPOSITE Meteorological Office weather map for Monday 5 June 1944, showing the deep depression centred off the north-east coast of the British Isles and resultant high winds in the English Channel, which forced Eisenhower to postpone the invasion by 24 hours.

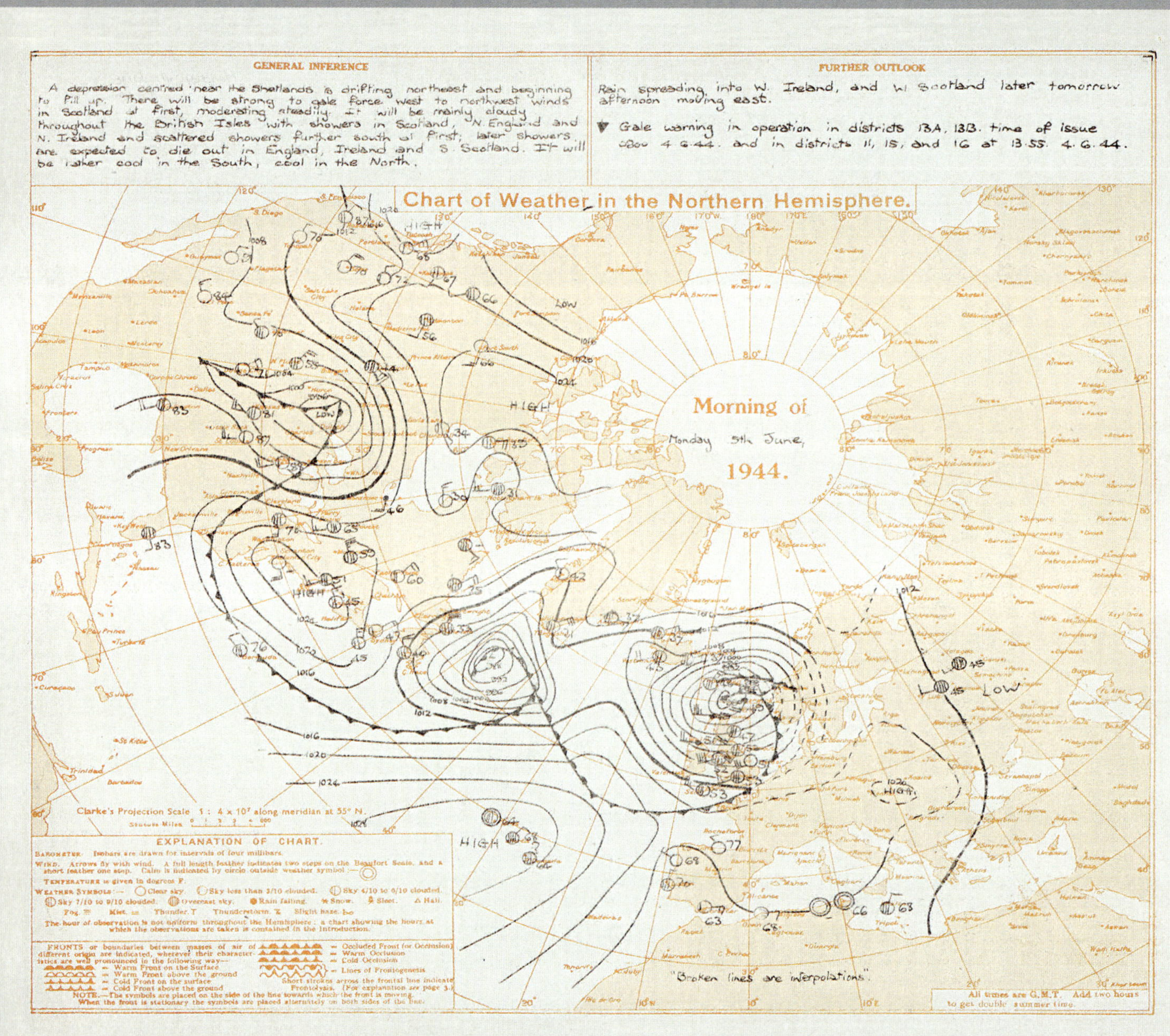

Page 4.

BRITISH SECTION

THE DAILY WEATHER REPORT OF THE METEOROLOGICAL OFFICE, AIR MINISTRY, LONDON.

Monday 5th June 1944

No 30146

OBSERVATIONS at 1hr. G.M.T. 5th June — OBSERVATIONS at 7hr. G.M.T. 5th June — PAST 24 HOURS.

Columns: District; Stations; Height above M.S.L. in feet; Barom. at M.S.L. mb. (1); Change in 3 hours (2); Wind: Direc. (3), Force (4); Weather (5); Temp. °F. (6); Dew Point °F. (7); Visibility 0–9 (8); Cloud: Form Low (9), Med. (10), High (11); Amount Total 0–9 (12), Low A. 0–9 (13), B. 0–9 (14); Height of Base Hundreds of feet A. (15), B. (16); Barom. at M.S.L. mb. (17); Change in 3 hours (18); Wind: Direc. (19), Force (20); Weather (21); Temp. °F. (22); Dew Point °F. (23); Visibility 0–9 (24); Cloud: Form Low (25), Med. (26), High (27); Amount Total 0–9 (28), Low A. 0–9 (29), B. 0–9 (30); Height of Base Hundreds of feet A. (31), B. (32); State of Ground 0–9 (33); Sea 0–9 (34); Temperature: Max. Day 7h–18h °F. (35), Min. Night 18h–7h °F. (36), Min. on Grass °F. (37); Rainfall: Day 7h–18h mm. (38), Night 18h–7h mm. (39); Sunshine Hrs. (40)

District	Stations	Height above M.S.L. in feet	Barom. at M.S.L. mb. (1)
1	Kew	16	
	Croydon	217	05·8
	Boscombe Down	417	10·1
	Thorney Island	10	10·7
	Friston	–	
	Lympne	341	10·1
	Manston	140	09·3
2	North Weald	244	10·0
	Felixstowe	10	08·5
	Gorleston	5	07·3
	Mildenhall	15	07·3
	Bircham Newton	221	06·4
	Cranwell	203	07·7
3	Cranfield	340	08·2
	Honiley	427	07·0
4	Little Rissington	731	08·2
	Shobden	318	07·0
5	Bristol	209	09·4
	Chivenor	20	10·6
	Yeovilton	50	1 ·3
	Portland Bill	32	12
	Exeter	100	11·5
	Plymouth	86	12·3
	St. Eval	345	12·4
	The Lizard	240	12·3
	Scilly, St. Marys	163	13·2
6	Fairwood	268	09·8
	Pembroke	142	07·2
	Aberporth	425	*
7	Penrhos	63	05·2
	Holyhead, Valley	32	03·7
	Hawarden	15	04·9
8	Manchester	230	04·1
	Squires Gate	30	02·1
	Silloth	25	01·5
9	Ashbourne	590	04·9
	Snaith	30	02·8
10	Spurn Head	29	03·4
	Catterick (Sc)	195	99·5
	Tynemouth	108	97·0
	Acklington	138	95·3
11	St. Abb's Head	280	92·5
	Leuchars	31	90·5
	Montrose	22	90·4
12	Abbotsinch	19	9[illegible]·5
	Prestwick	30	95·3
	West Freugh	53	97·3
	Eskdalemuir	794	*
	Jurby, I. of Man	84	99·0
13A	Machrihanish	35	95·3
	Tiree	44	92·0
	Oban	74	91·9
13B	Stornoway	12	84·2
	Cape Wrath	307	18·7
15	Dalwhinnie	1176	*
	Aberdeen†	79	88·0
	Fraserburgh	76	86·5
	Alness	63	85·0
	Wick	114	82·3
16	Hatston	45	80·8
	Sumburgh	15	81·9
	Sullom Voe	12	82·5
17	Blacksod Point	18	02·3
18	Malin Head	84	95·4
	Aldergrove	294	97·7
	Cas. Archdale	240	99·7
19	Birr Castle	173	*
	Collinstown	220	06·0
20	Foynes	3	16·4
	Valentia	30	16·4
	Roches Point	22	08·6

CODE FOR CLOUD AMOUNT (Cols. 12, 13, 14, 28, 29, 30).
0 = Nil; 1 = Trace; 2 = 1/10; 3 = 1/4; 4 = 1/2; 5 = 3/4; 6 = 9/10; 7 = More than 9 but with openings. 8 = Completely covered. 9 = Sky obscured by fog, etc.

Columns 13, 14, 15, 16, 29, 30, 31, 32. A = Lowest cloud present. B = Next lowest cloud.

* Information not usually received.
† 0h Observations from Dyce.
§ Sea disturbance reported from Dungeness.

NELSON K. JOHNSON, K.C.B., D.Sc., Director. Meteorological Office, Air Ministry, Kingsway, London, W.C.2.

THE BATTLE OF NORMANDY

WEDNESDAY 7 JUNE–FRIDAY 25 AUGUST 1944

The Battle of Normandy saw some of the toughest fighting in the Second World War. Some British and Canadian infantry battalions had casualties that exceeded those of the Battle of the Somme in 1916, despite overwhelming Allied air superiority. Much of the terrain favoured the German defenders – well-trained soldiers, equipped with superior tanks and the deadly shoulder-held *panzerfaust* anti-tank weapon.

The commander of the Allied armies in Normandy, General Sir Bernard Montgomery, planned to keep attacking on his left to draw in the bulk of the German armour, while the Americans on the right were to capture Cherbourg first, followed by turning around, smashing south through Mortain, out via Le Mans and on to the Seine. The burden of the grinding battles to pin the German armour was borne by the Canadians, British and the Polish Armoured Division. At times Montgomery was criticized by Churchill and Eisenhower, for lack of progress in these battles, particularly around Caen. But he stuck to his plan, and his confidence in Bradley's American soldiers was fully justified. By 27 June, Cherbourg was in their hands, and Bradley could now turn and start fighting south through the bocage, densest in the American sector. By 24 July, he had forced the Germans back and captured the key town of St Lô, and by 31 July, Avranches was in American hands. On 1 August, Lieutenant General George S. Patton's US Third Army, having arrived in Normandy, was unleashed to burst out towards Brittany, Nantes, Angers and Le Mans. A counter-attack by the German Seventh Army ordered by Hitler at Mortain was defeated between 6 and 10 August, and the expanding American torrent gathered momentum.

After bitter fighting, especially by the Poles and Canadians between Caen and Falaise, the remnants of 20 German divisions were pinned inside a pocket between Trun, Argentan and Chambois. Here, squeezed between the Polish Armoured Division and the Canadian II Corps on the north, the British XII and XXX Corps to the

ABOVE The battle for Caen. British infantry clearing snipers in Le Bijuale.

LIEUTENANT GENERAL OMAR BRADLEY *saw no active service in the First World War, becoming a protégé of General Marshall, the US Army Chief of Staff, before the Second. After commanding the US II Corps in Sicily under Patton, he was promoted over Patton's head when the latter was pilloried for slapping a soldier in hospital. Bradley was a painstaking commander of the US First Army in Normandy, and subsequently 12th Army Group, eventually commanding four armies, more troops than any other American in history.*

LEFT Badge of the US Third Army.

RIGHT Badge of the Ist Polish Armoured Division.

ABOVE After the break-out from Normandy, American infantry passing knocked-out German armour as they advance from St Lô, covering 97 miles in the first 10 days.

BELOW Death and destruction near Chambois in the Falaise Pocket. Allied air superiority turned roads in daylight into death traps for the Germans.

CHARLES DE GAULLE *as the leader of the Fighting French, again set foot on French soil on 14 June 1944, almost exactly four years after calling on Frenchmen everywhere to continue fighting. Like Churchill, de Gaulle was an indomitable character who came to personify his nation. On 25 August, with occasional shooting to be heard, he marched through Paris to a jubilant welcome, having told Eisenhower that unless he allowed Leclerc to liberate the city, he would order the move himself.*

west, and the US V Corps, which included the French 2nd Armoured Division, to the south, the Germans fought to stave off disaster. At one stage no less than three panzer divisions, attempting to relieve their trapped comrades, furiously attacked the Polish Armoured Division. The Poles, with a score to settle, resisted bitterly and suffered heavy casualties, but they succeeded in closing the pocket on 19 August.

MULBERRY *was the name given to two artificial harbours, each the size of Dover harbour, which were towed across the Channel: A for the Americans and B for the British. By taking their own harbours with them, allowing them to supply the beaches, the Allies fed the German belief that a major port or ports would have to be captured very early, and therefore the Pas de Calais must be the objective for the main Allied landing.*

ABOVE A Sherman tank rolls across the floating roadway connecting one of the piers of "Port Winston" to the beach at Arromanches.

ABOVE Excited crowds throng around a tank of General Leclerc's French 2nd Armoured Division as it drives into the heart of Paris on 25 August.

The Allied air forces hammered the pocket, causing huge casualties, and eventually resistance ceased. In a broad swathe the Allies advanced to the Seine, and crossed it at several points. Bradley planned to cross the Seine astride Paris and take the city by encirclement, avoiding fighting in the streets. The possibility of a Communist uprising in Paris, and Hitler's threat to burn the city brought matters to a head, and after an argument with Free French leader Charles de Gaulle, Eisenhower authorised troops to enter the city. The advance was led by General Jacques Leclerc's French 2nd Armoured Division. Considerable German resistance was encountered in the approaches to Paris, but at 9.30 p.m. on 24 August, Leclerc's leading elements had reached the Hotel de Ville, Major Jacques Massu being the first to salute the Unknown Warrior at the Arc de Triomphe.

The German commander finally surrendered to General Leclerc on the afternoon of 25 August.

The Allies had reached the Seine and Paris 10 days ahead of the 90 days forecast for the advance from the Normandy beachhead. Their success was costly: the Allied armies suffered 209,672 casualties including 36,976 dead between D-Day and crossing the Seine 77 days later. In addition, some 28,000 aircrew were lost in operations over France before D-Day and in the subsequent battle.

The battle for Normandy cost the Germans some 1,300 tanks, 3,500 guns, and 20,000 vehicles. More than 40 German divisions had been destroyed with the loss of 450,000 men, of which at least 50,000 were dead.

7 JUNE–25 AUGUST 1944

NORMANDY

KEY

Front line 14 August
Front line 19 August
Front line 25 August
German fortified areas

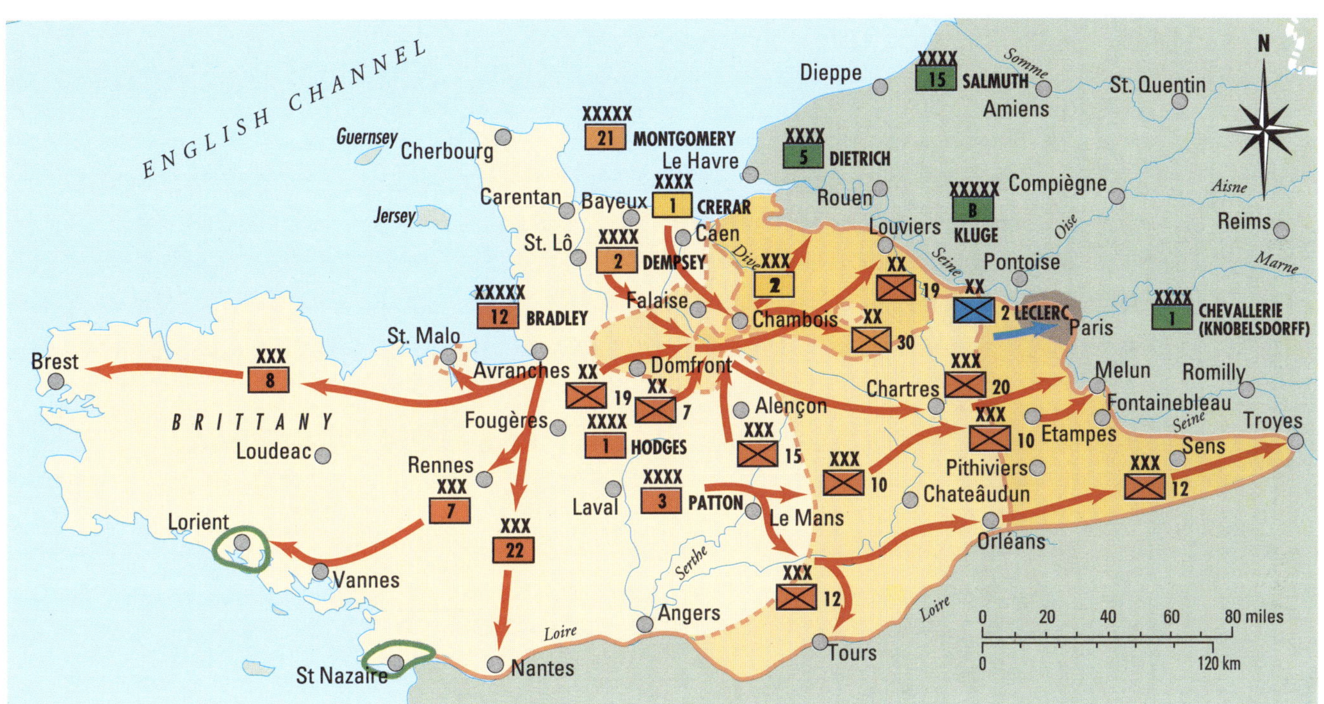

OPERATION DRAGOON

TUESDAY 15 AUGUST–FRIDAY 15 SEPTEMBER 1944

On 15 August, the 3rd and 36th Infantry Divisions of Major General Lucian Truscott's US VI Corps, part of Lieutenant General Alexander Patch's US Seventh Army, landed on the French Riviera between Cannes and Hyeres. To protect his flanks, a French Groupe de Commandos and the Canadian-American 1st Special Service Force landed on his left, while the Anglo/US 1st Airborne Task Force dropped at Le Muy. This Task Force included the 2nd Independent Parachute Brigade, the only British soldiers to take part in the operation, five US parachute battalions and one glider infantry regiment. Originally codenamed "Anvil", and eventually "Dragoon", the operation was originally planned as a feint to draw off troops during the Normandy landings, but at the behest of Eisenhower evolved into a major landing, albeit at the expense of the Italian Campaign. The number of troops involved needed so many landing craft (1,370) that the operation had to be postponed until these could be spared from Normandy.

BELOW Infantry landing down gang planks from an LCI in the South of France. The man on the ramp of the LCVP with jeep is acknowledging being called in to the beach.

OPERATION DRAGOON

ALLIES

US Seventh Army: Lt Gen Alexander Patch
US VI Corps landing on first day: Maj Gen Lucien Truscott

ASSAULT DIVISIONS ON THREE BEACHES:
H-Hour: 0700 hours
US 3rd Infantry Division (Alpha Beach)
US 45th Infantry Division (Delta Beach)
US 36th Infantry Division (Camel Beach)
French Commando Group landed on each flank

COMBINED US/BRITISH IST AIRBORNE TASK FORCE DZS (BETWEEN LA MOTTE AND LE MUY):
Major General Robert Frederick, US Army
Pathfinders: 03.34 hours
Main Drop: 04.45 hours

AXIS

DEFENDING:
Three divisions of General Blaskowitz's Army Group G

Before the landings five battleships, 21 cruisers and 100 destroyers bombarded the coast, supported by aircraft from seven British and two American carriers. A total of 887 warships and 1,370 landing craft participated. Opposing the landings were 10 German divisions of General Johannes Blaskowitz's Army Group C, of which only three were located near the beachhead. The Luftwaffe was outnumbered 10:1. Casualties were light on landing, and with the Allies about to cross the Seine further north, Hitler ordered his troops to withdraw rather than put up serious resistance.

On D+1, amid great emotion, seven French divisions of General Jean de Lattre de Tassigny's Army B (renamed First Army from 19 September) landed in the follow-up waves. ULTRA decrypts revealed that the Germans were not contemplating any serious counter-attacks against the landings and advance inland. So Truscott headed north for Avignon and Sisteron, while de Lattre's troops made for Toulon and Marseilles, both heavily defended fortresses. Toulon was taken on 21 August by the 9th Colonial Infantry Division (9e DIC). On 28 August, Marseilles fell to the Moroccan Goums and the Tirailleurs of the 3rd Algerian Infantry Division (3e DIA) fighting with great *élan*. The rapid capture of the two French ports was a brilliant feat of arms.

Meanwhile, Truscott, one of the best Allied generals, pressed on, and by the end of August was beyond Valence and Grenoble. The 11th Panzer Division fought hard at Montélimar to allow the better part of the German Nineteenth Army to escape, but Truscott reached Lyons by 3 September, and Besancon four days later.

ABOVE Follow-up waves of the Anglo/US 1st Airborne Task Force drop into the vineyards of southern France. Initial waves dropped at night.

LEFT Badge of the US Third Infantry Division.

MAJOR GENERAL LUCIAN TRUSCOTT *was one of the best Allied generals of the Second World War. He formed the first US Ranger battalion, and took part in the Dieppe raid; and commanded the US 3rd Infantry Division in Sicily, Salerno and Anzio where he took over command of the US VI Corps when General Lucas was sacked. He commanded the VI Corps for Operation Dragoon, before taking command of US Fifth Army in Italy, and leading it successfully for the rest of the war.*

15 AUGUST–15 SEPTEMBER 1944

OPERATION DRAGOON

LEFT American soldiers advance up the road away from the beachhead.

BELOW LEFT A souvenir bracelet showing the key actions of a US soldier's fight passing up through Italy: Naples, Anzio, Cassino and Rome. This bracelet was kept by French citizens who had buried the serviceman's body.

RIGHT French Commando badge.

De Lattre advanced up the west bank of the Rhône and Dijon fell to the French II Corps on 11 September. Here, a day later, a patrol from de Lattre's Army B met one from Leclerc's 2nd Armoured advancing from Normandy. Between 12 and 14 September at Dompaire near Epinal, Leclerc showed his tactical skill by so damaging 112 Panzer Brigade equipped with Tiger and Panther tanks, that it was unfit to take part in a planned attack.

On 15 September all Dragoon forces were switched from the Supreme Allied Commander, Mediterranean, General Sir Heny Maitland Wilson's command to Eisenhower's, and renamed Sixth Army Group.

That autumn, units formed from the Resistance (French Forces of the Interior – FFI), replaced large numbers of Armée d'Afrique (North and West African) soldiers in French First Army as it advanced towards the Vosges.

GENERAL JEAN DE LATTRE DE TASSIGNY

was wounded four times in the First World War (once by a lance in his chest), and again in Morocco. After commanding a division brilliantly in the Battle of France of 1940, he escaped from prison in Vichy France in 1943, and took command of French Army B (later First Army) in North Africa. He was a courageous, charismatic and skilled general, with a cavalryman's eye for terrain. Under his command First Army became famous for its "élan".

ABOVE A soldier of the 1st Free French Division of General de Monsabert's II Corps, gives the pretty girls of Dijon a smart eyes left as they pelt the soldiers with flowers.

ABOVE Adjutant Emile Lancery (left) of French II Corps advancing from the south, greets Sergeant Louis Basil from General Patton's US Third Army advancing from the north.

BELOW AND OPPOSITE Pages from full colour leaflet issued by the US War Information Office to French forces to help identify units and ranks of their American military partners in North-West Europe.

ARMÉE DE TERRE DES ÉTATS-UNIS

PARACHUTISTE ARMÉ DE CARABINE

FANTASSIN ARMÉ DE FUSIL ET DE BAÏONNETTE

CAPORAL (INF.) AVEC MASQUE À GAZ

Pilote
Pilot

Navigateur
Navigator

Bombardier
Bombardier

Membre d'équipage
Air Crew Member

"Ailes"

Les officiers, sous-officiers et soldats qui ont reçu une instruction spéciale ont droit au port des "ailes". Cet insigne se porte au-dessus de la poche supérieure gauche de la vareuse.

Mitrailleur d'aviation
Aerial Gunner

Pilote d'avion (senior)
Senior Pilot

Pilote d'aviation (vétéran)
Command Pilot

Pilote de planeur
Glider Pilot

Pilote d'aviation de transport
Service Pilot

Pilote de liaison
Liaison Pilot

Observateur d'aviation
Aircraft Observer

Observateur spécialisé
Technical Observer

Pilote de ballon
Balloon Pilot

Pilote de ballon (senior)
Senior Balloon Pilot

Médecin de l'armée de l'air
Flight Surgeon

Parachutiste
Parachutist

THE V-WEAPONS THREAT

Well before the Allied invasion of Normandy, which Hitler confidently expected to repulse, he developed a range of new weapons aimed at driving the British and Americans on the defensive, including flying-bombs and long-range rockets. The Germans called them *Vergeltunsgwaffen* (retaliation weapons, in revenge for the Allied bombing of German cities); they were known by the British as V-weapons.

HITLER'S V-WEAPONS

V-1 SPECIFICATIONS

Overall length of fuselage: 7.23m (23' 8")
Overall length including engine: 7.90 m (25' 11")
Wing span: 5.38 m (17' 8")
Weight at launch: 2150 kg (4,740 lb)
of which warhead: 830 kg (1,830 lb)
fuel: 550 kg (1,212 lb)
Maximum range: 230 km (143 miles)
Maximum velocity 644 km/h (402 mph)

V-2 SPECIFICATIONS

Length: 14 m (45' 11")
Diameter of main body: 1.65 m (5' 5")
Weight at launch: 12.7 tonnes
of which fuel: 3.9 tonnes
lox (liquid oxygen): 5 tonnes
warhead: 1 tonne
Thrust at liftoff: 25 tonnes
Maximum burning time: 65 seconds
Maximum velocity: 5760 km/h (3580 mph) at engine cut-off
Apogee: 29,520 ft
Maximum range: 320 km (200 miles)

The V-1, or "flying bomb", was a small pilotless aircraft with a warhead, powered by a pulse-jet engine. It could be launched from a sloping ramp or dropped from a specially adapted bomber. The first experimental flight was made from Peenemünde, on the Baltic, under the supervision of Wernher von Braun in December 1942. In August 1943, conscript workers began the 96 V-1 launching sites mainly in the Pas de Calais area. Allied bombing slowed down construction drastically, but on 13 June 1944, seven days after D-Day in Normandy, the first V-1 hit London. By the end of the month, 2,452 had been launched against England. About 800 landed on London; around a third of them crashed or were shot down by fighters or anti-aircraft guns before they reached the coast, while another third crashed or were shot down over southern England. The air-launched version was less successful, mainly because the launching bombers were intercepted by RAF night fighters.

LEFT A flying bomb being pushed up its launching ramp. The wings were less than halfway back down the fuselage from the nose; the explosive warhead was situated between the second white ring and the wings.

"We are at present devoting nearly 50% of our air effort in trying to stop these beastly bombs, added to which about 25% of London's production is lost through the result of these bombs!"

FIELD MARSHAL SIR ALAN BROOKE, CHIEF OF THE IMPERIAL GENERAL STAFF COMMENTING ON V-1S IN HIS DIARY

The V-1 attacks on London persisted until the end of March 1945, with interruptions caused by fuel shortages. From October 1944, Belgian cities were also attacked with V-1s, especially the vital supply port of Antwerp, which suffered considerable damage. Over 10,000 V-1s were eventually launched against England, of which over 7,000 crossed the coast, and nearly 4,000 were shot down. The majority were aimed at London, although a few reached Southampton and Portsmouth, and one hit Manchester. The V-1s caused 6,184 deaths and injured 17,981.

The sound of the flying bomb's engine, which could be heard from the ground, led to it being nicknamed the "doodlebug" or "buzz bomb". At the end of its flight, the engine cut out, and the weapon plunged to earth, exploding on impact. If one was close enough to hear the engine cut out, one knew the impact area was nearby. This was nerve-wracking enough. Far worse was the V-2 rocket. The first intimation of its arrival was a huge explosion.

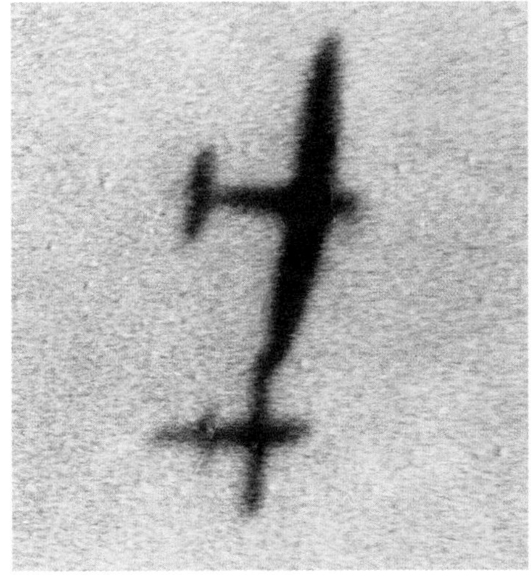

ABOVE Flight Sergeant Rose, a Tempest pilot and the first to shoot down a flying bomb, draws a sketch of the weapon for other pilots.

LEFT A Spitfire flies up alongside a V-1 flying bomb and flicks it over with its wingtip.

LEFT An injured man is rescued after a V-1 attack on London in June 1944. V-1 attacks persisted until the end of March 1945, and claimed over 6,000 lives.

The first V-2 to hit London exploded in Chiswick on 8 September 1944, killing three people and injuring 20. Antwerp also came under attack from V-2s, taking 900 hits during the last quarter of 1944. V-2 attacks persisted to within a month of the end of the war in Europe, with England receiving an average of five attacks per day, including three aimed at London. Over 2,700 Londoners were killed in total.

The main effect of the V-weapons, especially the V-2, was on morale. The south-east of England, having endured the Blitz, became increasingly nervous of these weapons plunging from the sky without warning. Although the RAF and USAAF hunted for the launchers, the V-2 sites in particular were hard to find. The rocket with its launch gear was easily transported, and it required only a small concrete pad as a firing platform. The one sure means of bringing the attacks to a stop was by ground forces overrunning all the sites in the course of the Allied advance into Holland and Germany, and it took until March 1945 to achieve this.

ABOVE A V-2 Rocket being prepared for launching from a forest pad. This picture illustrates the difficulty of finding launching sites from the air.

The V-2 was a ballistic missile powered by a rocket motor – the predecessor of today's intercontinental rockets. It was first fired successfully in October 1942, but because of its size and complexity, operational production at the vast underground factory at Nordhausen in the Harz Mountains did not begin until May 1944. This site was chosen because Peenemünde had earlier come under heavy attack from the RAF and USAAF.

FREIHERR WERNHER VON BRAUN

became technical director of the German rocket project at Peenemünde in 1937. His early work bore fruit when Hitler ordered production of the V-2 in 1943. He survived an RAF attack on Peenemünde, and arrest by the SS when Himmler tried to take over the programme. In March 1945, with 100 of his staff, he escaped ahead of the advancing Red Army. They eventually went to the USA and became a vital part of the American space programme.

ABOVE The Peenemünde rocket experimental facility taken in June 1943 and the same rocket site after heavy pounding by bombers.

BELOW Sketches and mathematical calculations carried out by Wernher von Braun in Peenemünde.

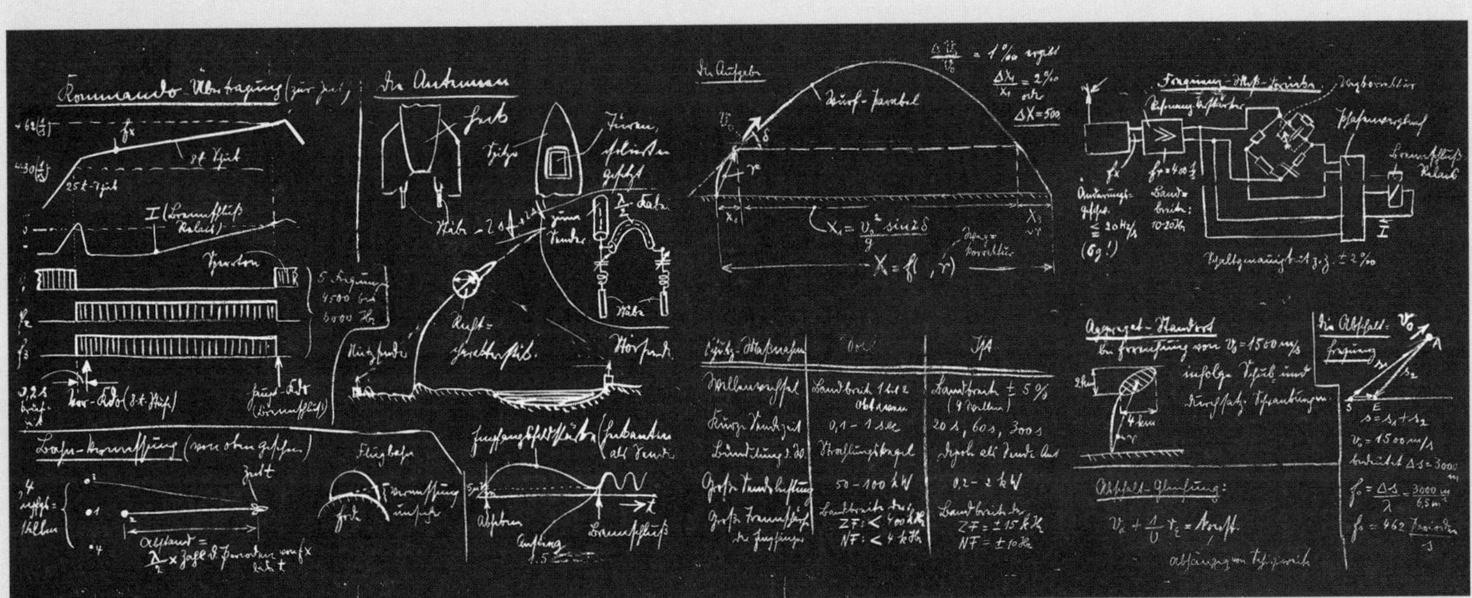

TO THE BORDERS OF THE REICH

SATURDAY 26 AUGUST–SATURDAY 16 SEPTEMBER 1944

On 26 August 1944, the Allied Armies were on the line of the River Seine, the British and Canadian 21st Army Group on the left, and the US 12th Army Group on the right. By 4 September, in a lightning advance, Montgomery had driven his armour forward 250 miles in a week taking Brussels and Antwerp.

Especially satisfying was the liberation of Dieppe on 1 September, where the Canadians had suffered terrible losses in the raid just over two years earlier. The day before, the British 11th Armoured Division entered Amiens having driven 60 miles in 48 hours. The Guards Armoured Division liberated Brussels to wild scenes of jubilation. The 11th Armoured Division swept into Antwerp so rapidly the Germans did not have time to blow the harbour sluice gates and dockside equipment. The Canadians advancing along the coast cleared the Pas de Calais of enemy except the garrisons besieged in Boulogne, Calais and Dunkirk. On 10 September the 51st (Highland) and 49th Divisions attacked Le Havre, after a bombardment by the Navy and several attacks by RAF Bomber Command. After 48 hours of fighting, one of the strongest fortresses of the Atlantic Wall fell. Major General Percy Hobart's "funnies" (specially adapted tanks for engineering tasks) of his 79th Division played a leading part in overcoming the concrete defences, minefields and obstacles.

LEFT Canadian First Army badge.

BELOW Citizens of Dieppe watch troops of Canadian 2nd Division march with ceremony into the town where this same division had suffered so grievously in the raid on 19 August 1942.

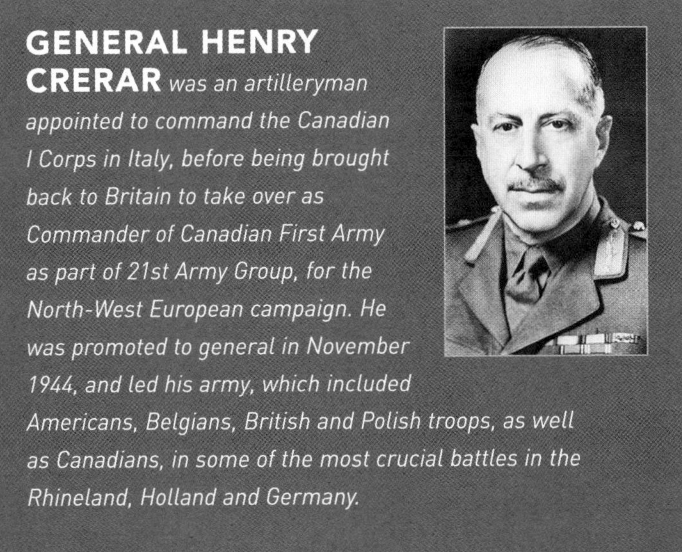

GENERAL HENRY CRERAR *was an artilleryman appointed to command the Canadian I Corps in Italy, before being brought back to Britain to take over as Commander of Canadian First Army as part of 21st Army Group, for the North-West European campaign. He was promoted to general in November 1944, and led his army, which included Americans, Belgians, British and Polish troops, as well as Canadians, in some of the most crucial battles in the Rhineland, Holland and Germany.*

ABOVE A Daimler armoured car of B Squadron, 2nd Household Cavalry Regiment, Guards Armoured Division drives through the streets of newly liberated Brussels.

ABOVE Flail tanks of the 22nd Dragoons and flame-thrower "Crocodiles" of 141st Regiment Royal Armoured Corps advance on Le Havre.

By 13 September, Lieutenant General Brian Horrocks' XXX Corps had seized a crossing over the Meuse-Escaut Canal, a necessary step before Montgomery's push to the Rhine and beyond – Operation Market Garden.

Meanwhile Patton's Third Army had advanced to the Meuse at Verdun, where it halted for lack of fuel. When trucks appeared carrying rations, he shouted at Bradley, "I'll shoot the next man who brings me food. Give us gasoline; we can eat our belts." For logistic reasons Eisenhower, who had taken over from Montgomery as the overall land commander, gave priority to Montgomery's British and Canadian 21st Army Group in the north, because he wanted the Pas de Calais cleared, and Antwerp captured to shorten supply lines. But Patton, supported by Bradley, badgered Eisenhower to allow him

ABOVE The people of Brussels give British and Belgian troops a tremendous welcome.

LIEUTENANT GENERAL MILES DEMPSEY *commanded a company at 19 and was awarded the Military Cross aged 23. He commanded a brigade at Dunkirk, and the XIII Corps in Egypt, Sicily and Italy, before being brought back to England to take over British Second Army for Normandy. The success enjoyed by Second Army was largely due to his first-class planning and leadership. A self-effacing man who shunned publicity, he mistakenly gave people the impression that Montgomery ran Second Army, which was by no means the case.*

ABOVE RIGHT An American military policeman directs trucks of the "Red Ball Express" taking supplies forward.

LEFT British 11th Armoured Division badge.

to push on and attack the Siegfried Line – the defensive network defending Germany's western border. The wily Patton did not reveal to Eisenhower that one of his corps had captured enough fuel to advance to the Moselle. Eisenhower gave in, a great mistake, because by spreading his logistic resources, he risked weakening both army groups, and achieving neither the capture and opening of Antwerp nor the reaching of the Siegfried Line.

The Allied victory in Normandy had produced a supply nightmare as the armies had advanced far quicker than planned for by logisticians. There was no lack of supplies available; the problem was caused by the need to move ammunition, food and fuel all the way from Normandy to the Allied armies dashing across France and into Belgium. To resolve the situation, the Americans started the "Red Ball Express". Some 6,000 trucks drove around the clock along a one-way road system connecting Normandy to the front. Although hallowed by myth, the Red Ball delivered a fraction of the supplies needed, while wearing out trucks and drivers, and itself using 300,000 gallons of fuel a day – nearly enough to supply an army.

LEFT American infantry crossing the border between Belgium and Germany near Aachen on 12 September 1944.

26 AUGUST–16 SEPTEMBER 1944

TO THE BORDERS OF THE REICH

KEY

Front line 26 August
Front line 17 September
Siegfried Line (Westwall)

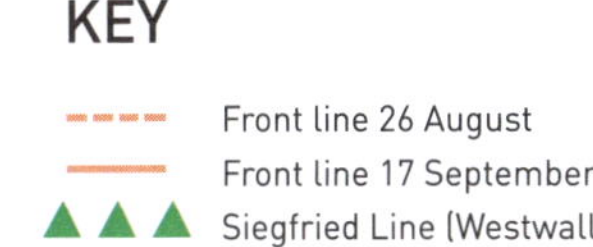

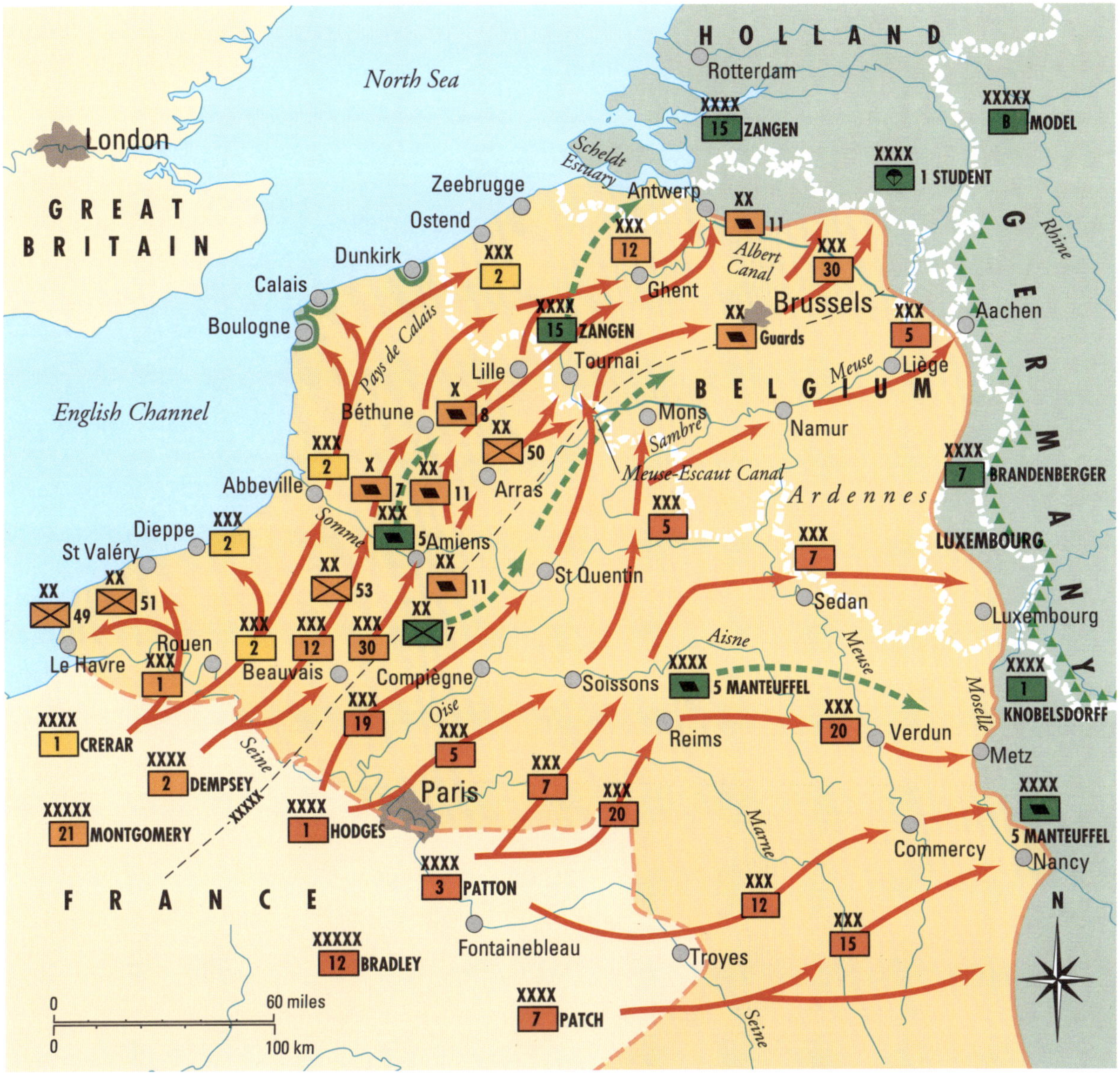

MARKET GARDEN: THE DROP

SUNDAY 17 SEPTEMBER 1944

On 9 September, Eisenhower rejected Montgomery's proposal that the Allies advance to Berlin in a single thrust, but conceded that his flank should have priority for supplies. He had also placed the American Lieutenant General Lewis Brereton's First Allied Airborne Army in support of Montgomery.

After the fall of Antwerp, Montgomery planned to cross the Rhine at Arnhem, advance east towards Osnabruck, Munster and Hamm, and along the eastern face of the Ruhr, the industrial heart of Germany, with the aim of bringing the war to an end in the winter of 1944. Between Dempsey's British Second Army on the Meuse-Escaut Canal and the far bank of the Rhine, lay three broad canals and three great rivers; from south to north, the Wilhelmina Canal, the Zuid Wilhelmina Canal, the River Maas, the Maas-Waal Canal, the River Waal and the Lower Rhine.

ABOVE Parachute soldiers of the British 1st Airborne Division just before emplaning in C-47 Dakotas for the drop on Arnhem.

BELOW Paratroopers of the 101st US Airborne Division rigging up by their C-47 Dakotas on an airfield in England, before their drop near Eindhoven.

MARKET GARDEN

ALLIES

BRITISH I AIRBORNE CORPS:
Lt Gen Frederick Browning
British 1st Airborne Division
US 82nd Airborne Division
US 101st Airborne Division
1st Polish Parachute Brigade Group

AIRLIFT:
British: 564 parachute aircraft, 670 tug aircraft and 670 gliders
US: 981 parachute aircraft, 478 tug aircraft and 478 gliders

TOTAL ALLIED AIRBORNE CASUALTIES:
British: 7,167 (including 6,584 POWs)
US: 3,532

AXIS

FIRST PARACHUTE ARMY GEN KURT STUDENT UNDER COMMAND AT OUTSET:
176th Infantry Division
Parachute Training Division
Battle Group Walter
85th Infantry Division
719th Infantry Division

REINFORCEMENTS:
59th Infantry Division
17th Panzer Brigade
9th SS Panzer Division
10th SS Panzer Division

ABOVE First Allied Airborne Army badge.

ABOVE British paratroopers boarding a C-47 Dakota. Unlike US paratroopers, the British did not use a reserve parachute. Wearing the haversack under the jump smock accounts for the "pregnant" appearance.

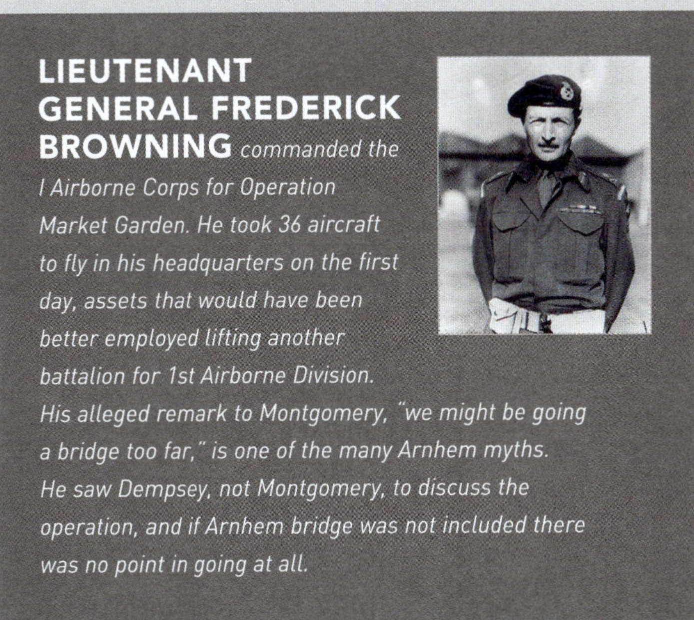

LIEUTENANT GENERAL FREDERICK BROWNING *commanded the I Airborne Corps for Operation Market Garden. He took 36 aircraft to fly in his headquarters on the first day, assets that would have been better employed lifting another battalion for 1st Airborne Division. His alleged remark to Montgomery, "we might be going a bridge too far," is one of the many Arnhem myths. He saw Dempsey, not Montgomery, to discuss the operation, and if Arnhem bridge was not included there was no point in going at all.*

Dempsey planned to use First Allied Airborne Army to lay an airborne carpet across the waterways, and seize a bridgehead north of Arnhem. I Airborne Corps, commanded by the British Lieutenant General Frederick Browning, consisting of 82nd and 101st US; 1st British Airborne Divisions provided the troops. The canal crossings between Eindhoven and Veghel were allocated to Major General Maxwell Taylor's 101st. The bridges over the Maas, the Waal, and the Maas-Waal Canal were the objectives of Major General James Gavin's 82nd. Major General Robert Urquhart's British 1st Airborne was given the most distant objective, the bridge over the Lower Rhine at Arnhem.

In the van of Second Army advancing across the airborne carpet would be Horrocks's XXX Corps, consisting of Guards Armoured Division, and 43rd (Wessex) and 50th Infantry Divisions. Horrocks would have XI Corps on his left and VIII Corps on his right. The codename for the airborne operation was "Market" and for the ground advance "Garden".

There were insufficient aircraft to bring all three airborne divisions in complete on day one of the operation, so follow-up lifts were planned for succeeding days. Two lifts could have been achieved on the first day if Brereton had seen fit to fly the first in darkness. The airborne plan was driven by the airmen and additionally flawed by

17–30 SEPTEMBER 1944

OPERATION MARKET GARDEN

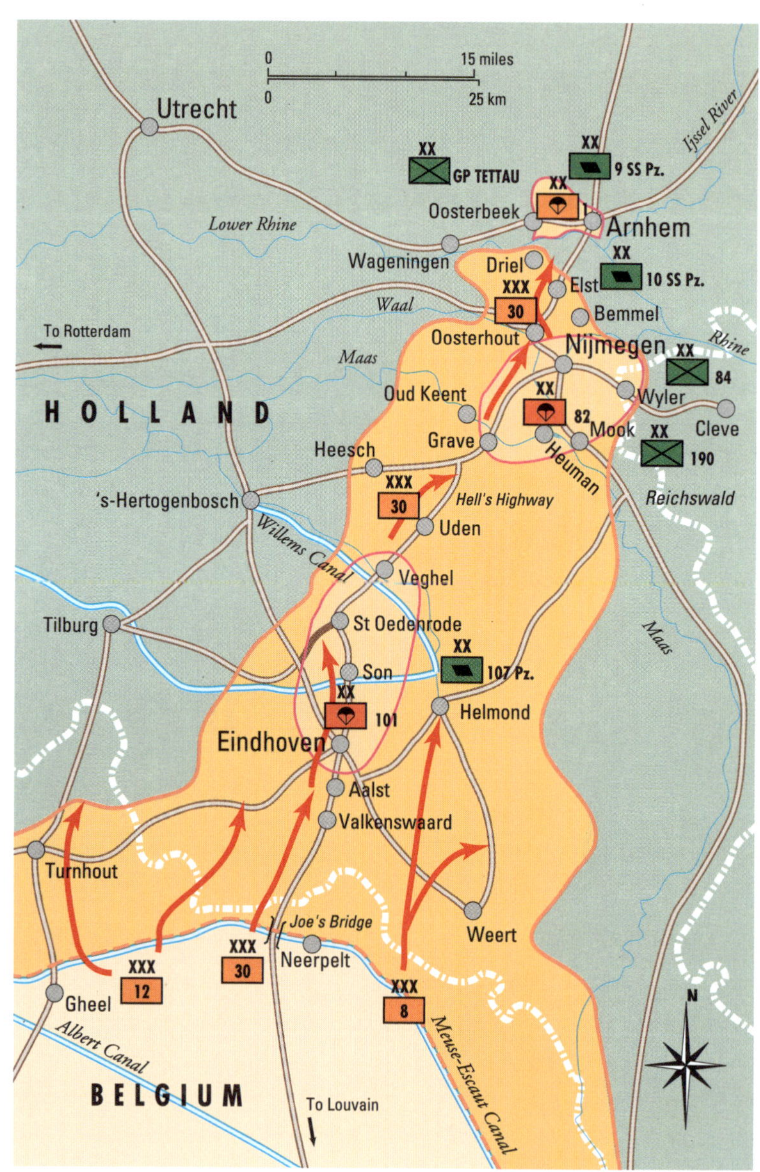

KEY

Front line 16 September

Front line 30 September

Allied drop zones

failure to land on both sides of some of the major water obstacles, and by selecting many drop and landing zones (DZs and LZs) too far from the objectives. Brereton would not countenance landing by night and especially night coup de main operations by gliders, so successful in Normandy three months before.

At lunch time on Sunday 17 September the first aircraft of an air armada of 1,534 troop-carrying aircraft, and 491 gliders and tugs passed over the Oosterbeek headquarters of Field Marshal Walther Model, the commander of Army Group B, where he was having a glass of wine. They were carrying the first lift of the three airborne divisions, taking off from 22 airfields in England. Nearly 35,000 airborne soldiers would be lifted to battle on this and succeeding days. The landings of the leading elements of all three divisions were carried out against negligible opposition, and the airborne soldiers headed for their objectives.

Model sped off to find the commander of the understrength II SS Panzer Corps, Lieutenant General Wilhelm Bittrich. Many of Bittrich's units, all located over 20 miles north-east of Arnhem, were due to leave for Germany that day – some were on trains. Bittrich worked with lightning speed and despatched a battle group of 9th SS Panzer Division to the British drop zones and landing zones west of Oosterbeek. The rest of 9th SS, a division in name only, set up blocking positions west of Arnhem. Bittrich ordered 10th SS Panzer Division to seize the Nijmegen Bridge, and halt or delay the link-up forces to give him time to destroy the British Airborne, with the help of reinforcements from Army Group B.

ABOVE Landing zone Z at Arnhem with gliders that have brought in anti-tank guns, Reconnaissance Squadron and 1st Parachute Brigade vehicles, light artillery and divisional troops.

LEFT Glider Pilot Regiment badge.

ABOVE A follow-up wave of paratroopers of the 82nd Airborne Division drop at Grave into a drop zone where WACO gliders had landed earlier.

ABOVE RIGHT Villagers of Valkenswaard, south of Eindhoven, watching Allied tug aircraft and gliders passing overhead on their way to landing zones further north.

ABOVE A two-and-a-half Guilder note, printed in the USA, used by Allied troops in liberated Holland.

STATE OF INFORMATIONS for the Dutch, to help the Allied Forces.
STAAT VAN INLICHTINGEN voor Nederlanders, inzake hulp aan de Geallieerde Strijdkrachten.

== ==

ATTENTION! Soldiers, show the list-number to the Dutchmen and they will tell you what you need with gesticulations, etc.
ATTENTIE! Soldaten, wijs het lijst-nummer aan en de Nederlanders zullen U zeggen wat U noodig hebt, in gebarentaal, enz.

I. Questions about the enemy.
Vragen over den vijand.

II. Questions about the surroundings.
Vragen over de omgeving.

III. Questions about the municipal position.
Vragen over gemeentelijke toestanden.

IV. Questions about personal needs.
Vragen over persoonlijke behoeften.

--- ---

Yes (spreek uit: jes, als in flesch) = ja
No (spreek uit: noo, als in noot) = neen
I (ai) don't (doont) know (noow) = Ik weet het niet.

--- ---

I. Questions about the enemy.
Vragen over den vijand.

1) Where are the Germans?
Waar zijn de Duitschers?

a) in the direction of my hand.
in de richting van mijn hand (wijs met Uw hand aan)

b) I'll show you the way.
Ik zal U den weg wijzen.

2) Accompany us . . . . Yes/No
Ga met ons mee . . . . Ja /Neen

3) Is here German infantry? . . . . Yes/No
Is hier Duitsche infanterie? . . . . Ja /Neen

4) Is here German artillery?. . . . . Yes/No
Is hier Duitsche artillerie? . . . . Ja /neen

5) Is here an airfield? . . . . Yes/No
Is hier een vliegveld? . . . . Ja /neen

6) Are here tanks? . . . . Yes/NO
Zijn hier tanks? . . . . Ja/ Neen

7) Are here German strongholds? . . . . . . Yes/No
Zijn hier Duitsche versterkingen? . . . . Ja /Neen

8) Where are places with landmines? . . . . Please follow me.
Waar zijn plaatsen met landmijnen? . . . . Gaat U maar mee.

9) Is here a German garrison in this city/village? . . Yes/No
Is er een Duitsch garnisoen in deze stad/dorp? . . Ja /Neen

10) Are here war-factories? . . . . Yes/No
Zijn hier fabrieken v. oorlogsindustrie? . . . . . . Ja /Neen

2.

II. Questions about the surroundings.
Vragen over de omgeving.

1) Where are we? . . . . You are in ....
Waar zijn wij? . . . . U bent in ....(vul in)

2) Where is the coast?
Waar is de kust?

3) Where is the harbour?
Waar is de haven?

4) Is this the way to the airfield of the Hague, Amsterdam, etc.?
Is dit de weg naar het vliegveld van den Haag, Amsterdam, enz.?

5) Where is the headway to the Hague, Rotterdam, Utrecht, etc.?
Waar loopt de hoofdweg naar den Haag,Rotterdam,Utrecht,enz.?

a) in the direction of my hand
in de richting van mijn hand (wijs aan)

b) I'll show you the way.
Ik zal U den weg wijzen.

6) Where is the river Rhine, Meuse, etc.?
Waar loopt de Rijn, de Maas, enz.?

7) Please, show me the shortest way to the railway-station.
Wijst U mij de kortste weg naar het spoorweg-station.

a) Please, follow me.
Gaat U maar met me mee.

8) Show me please the shortest way to the ferry-bOat, to the bridge.
Wijst U mij de kortste weg naar de veerpont, naar de brug.

9) There lives a Nazi.
Daar woont een Nazi (wijs aan)

10) There is a prison, a concentrationcamp.
Daar is een gevangenis, een concentratiekamp.

=--- ---=

III. Questions about the municipal position.
Vragen over de gemeentelijke toestanden.

1) Tell me please the way tot the townhall . . . Please follow me.
Wijst U mij a.u.b. de weg naar 't stadhuis. . Gaat U maar mee.

2) Where is the burgomaster? . . . . Please follow me.
Waar vind ik de burgemeester? . . . . Gaat U maar mee.

3) Where is the police-station?. . . . . Please follow me.
Waar is het politie-bureau? . . . . Gaat U maar mee.

4) Are here public-buildings? . . . . . . Yes/No / I don't know.
Zijn hier openbare gebouwen?. . . . . . Ja /Neen/Ik weet 't niet.

a) Where are the public-waterworks?
Waar is het waterleidingbedrijf?

b) Where are the gas-works?
Waar is de gasfabriek?

c) Where is the electric-powerstation?
Waar is het electriciteitsbedrijf?

d) Where is the post-office? . . . . Please follow me.
Waar is het postkantoor? . . . . Gaat U maar mee.

e) Where is the telephone/telegraph-office?.
Waar is het telefoon/telegraaf-kantoor?

ABOVE Translation aid produced and distributed throughout the Dutch Resistance network to help their members work with liberating Allied forces.

RIGHT Top-secret list of password challenges and responses issued to commanding officers of troop carrier squadrons by HQ Troop Carrier Group the day before the first drop. The same passwords were used by British First Airborne Division in Arnhem. The planners had assumed five days' worth of passwords would be sufficient. In the event, they would need nine.

Reg. No. TS-313

Copy No. 3

T O P S E C R E T

TOP SECRET
Auth: Co, 314th TC Gp
Date: 16 Sept. 1944
Init: WPR

HEADQUARTERS
314TH TROOP CARRIER GROUP, AAF
APO 133

16 September, 1944.

SUBJECT: Passwords for "MARKET" Mission.

TO : Commanding Officers, 32nd Troop Carrier Squadron
50th Troop Carrier Squadron
61st Troop Carrier Squadron
62nd Troop Carrier Squadron

Att: Intelligence Officers.

1. Passwords for "MARKET" Mission are as follows:

	CHALLENGE	REPLY
H-Hour through 2359, D-Day	Red	Beret
2359, D-Day through 2359, D & 1	Uncle	Sam
2359, D & 1 " 2359, D & 2	Carrier	Pigeon
2359, D & 2 " 2359, D & 3	Aire	Borne
2359, D & 3 " 2359, D & 4	Robert	Burns
2359, D & 4 " 2359, D & 5	Troop	Carrier

By order of Colonel STILES:

for William P. Ryan
W. J. CARMICHAEL,
Capt, AC,
Adjutant.

- 1 -

T O P S E C R E T

MARKET GARDEN: TO NIJMEGEN

SUNDAY 17–THURSDAY 21 SEPTEMBER 1944

The first link-up by XXX Corps driving north to Arnhem was with the US 101st Airborne Division, but even at this early stage Horrocks, having to fight along a one-road axis against unexpectedly stubborn German resistance, was 24 hours late. The Germans blew the bridge over the Wilhelmina Canal at Zon in the face of the US 506th Parachute Infantry Regiment. There were further delays while Bailey bridging was brought up from the rear of the column through the massive crowds packing the streets of Eindhoven.

The US 101st had taken the bridge at Veghel intact, but the leading elements of XXX Corps did not cross it and enter Uden until 19 September, by which time they should have reached the British I Airborne at Arnhem, but still had 29 miles to cover, nearly half the total distance of 64 miles. The US 82nd Airborne Division captured the bridges over the Maas at Grave and Maas-Waal Canal intact, and headed for Nijmegen. No plans had been made to drop in the vicinity of the great road bridge over the Waal. Browning's order to Gavin to take and hold the Groesbeek Heights against the possibility of a German counter-attack in this vicinity, although there was no intelligence that there were any enemy in the area, was an unwelcome diversion from the US 82nd's main mission of securing Nijmegen. Browning had further complicated matters by siting British I Airborne Corps headquarters there and taking 36 aircraft to fly the HQ in – aircraft which would have been better employed taking in more of British 1st Airborne Division on day one.

US 82nd Airborne sent patrols into Nijmegen, found it lightly held to begin with, but by the time a probe in strength was made on 20 September, the Germans had moved into the town and the

LEFT Nijmegen Bridge on 21 September, the day after its capture. Guards Armoured Division is streaming past a wrecked German army bus. By now the Arnhem bridge was back in German hands.

ABOVE US 82nd Airborne Division badge.

ABOVE A Bren gun carrier and other transport cross the Nijmegen bridge towards Arnhem.

LEFT British XXX Corps badge.

ABOVE Tanks of the 2nd Battalion (Armoured) Grenadier Guards crossing the Nijmegen Bridge captured by the battalion the evening before.

ABOVE "Hell's Highway" between Eindhoven and Nijmegen. US paratroopers take cover while British transport hit by German self-propelled guns blows up.

LIEUTENANT GENERAL BRIAN HORROCKS *was very much a "Monty man". He was a successful corps commander in North Africa, where he was badly wounded. Montgomery brought him over to France to take over XXX Corps. An inspiring leader with humour and charm, Market Garden was the one exception to his long record of battle successes. Underneath his confident air, Horrocks had considerable doubts about the plan, remarking to Gavin during the battle, "never try to fight an entire corps off one road".*

BRIGADIER GENERAL JIM GAVIN

known as "Slim Jim" to his soldiers, was a tough ex-ranker, and, at 37, the youngest divisional commander in the US Army; he was promoted to Major General while on the operation. He had led the 505th Parachute Infantry Regiment in Sicily and Italy.

Browning's interference in Gavin's plans to seize the Nijmegen Bridge on the second day of the operation was an important reason for the failure to relieve British 1st Airborne at Arnhem; not insisting on drop zones each side of the Waal was another.

Huner Park to the south. Because no plan had been made to land on both sides of the Waal, the US 504th Parachute Infantry was ordered to cross the river in boats. Their crossing was delayed until the Grenadier Guards, the leading battle group of XXX Corps, and American paratroopers cleared the Huner Park and the town of Nijmegen. This took all morning of 20 September. That afternoon, the US 504th launched their boats into the fast running 400-yard wide river. With sublime courage the American paratroopers paddled across in the face of heavy fire, eventually managing to obtain a foothold on the far bank. From here, they headed for the northern end of the road bridge. On the way they took the railway bridge over the river, and the Grenadiers on the south bank, seeing the American flag being raised, sent five tanks across the road bridge and met the Americans advancing from the other direction.

But the road to Arnhem was still not open. German armour, hitherto prevented by British 1st Airborne Division from crossing and heading south, was racing to block the route.

LEFT British infantry and armour of VII Corps advancing on the right of XXX Corps, approach the village of Asten, with some infantry riding on a tank.

17–21 SEPTEMBER 1944

NIJMEGEN

KEY

Front line 17 September

Front line 21 September

Parachute drop zone

Glider landing zone

0 8 miles
0 5 km
N
To Arnhem
Waal
III 504
II GREN GDS
Groesbeek Heights
Maas-Waal Canal
Nijmegen
III 504
Honinghutje
II 1/505
Beek
XX 84
Berg-en-Dal
III 508
Wyler
III 508
Hatert
Alverna
III 504
XX 82
II 1/505
III 508
XXX 1AB HQ
Nederasselt
Malden
Groesbeek
III 504
III 504
III 325
Grave
Overasselt
Heumen
Molenhoek
Maas
XXX 30
Mook
III 505
Reichswald
To Eindhoven
Cuijk
Riethorst
XX 190

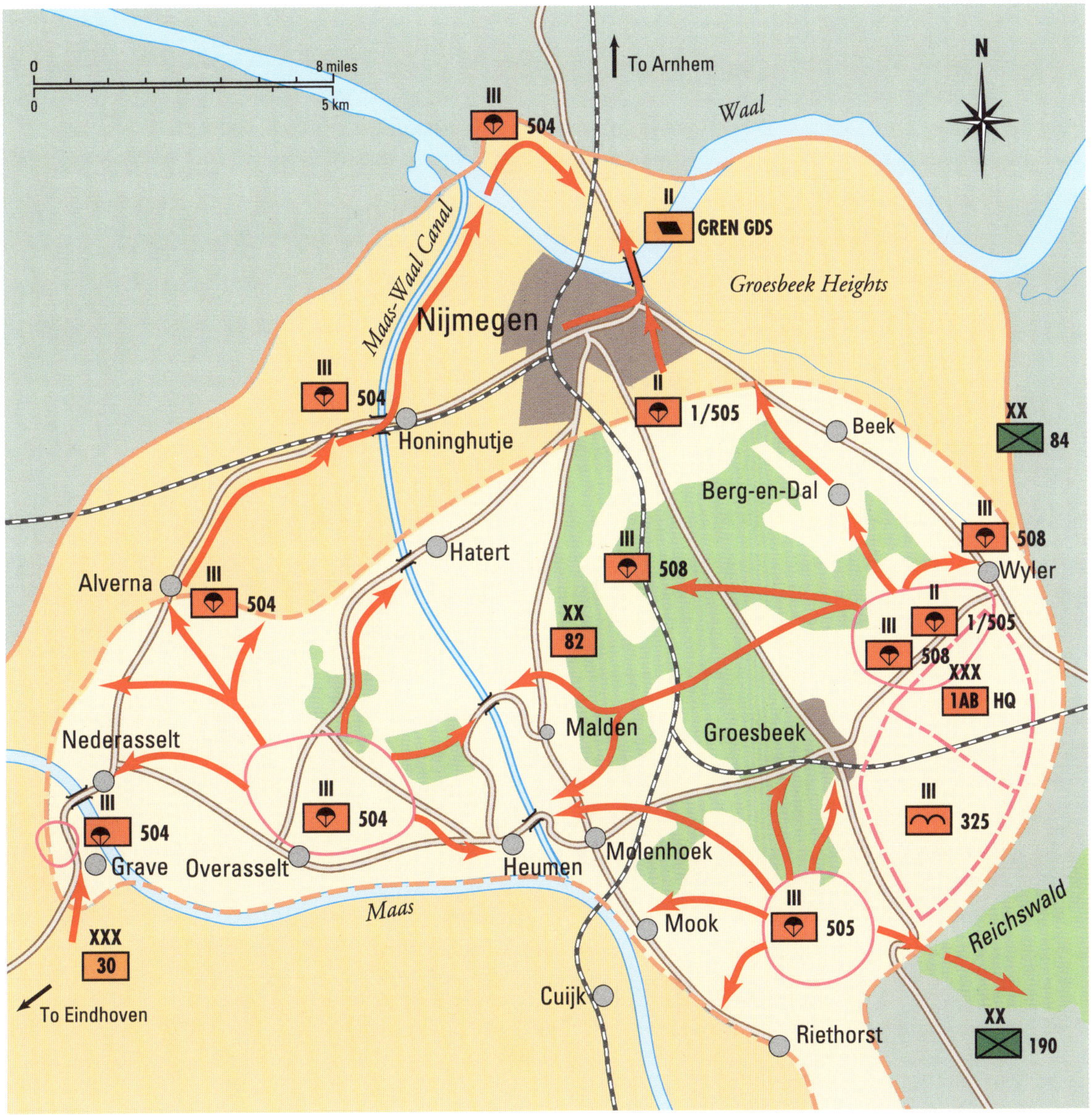

MARKET GARDEN: ARNHEM

SUNDAY 17–TUESDAY 26 SEPTEMBER 1944

First to arrive on the British 1st Airborne Division drop zone west of Arnhem was Brigadier Gerald Lathbury's 1st Parachute Brigade and the Divisional Reconnaissance Squadron. General Urquhart sent the Squadron ahead in jeeps to seize the Arnhem Bridge. They ran into SS Major Krafft's panzer grenadier training battalion that happened to be stationed nearby and were cut to pieces.

Brigadier Lathbury despatched his three parachute battalions to the Arnhem Bridge on three separate routes. Only the 2nd Battalion commanded by Lieutenant Colonel John Frost, approaching on a road alongside the river, reached the bridge in the early evening of Sunday 17th. The battalion attempted to cross and capture the southern end, but was beaten back. Frost's men held houses on the northern side, preventing the Germans from using the bridge.

LIEUTENANT COLONEL JOHN FROST *led the raid on Bruneval, and subsequently commanded 2nd Parachute Battalion in North Africa, Sicily and Italy before taking it to Arnhem. Following the southernmost route, on Sunday evening he occupied houses dominating the northern end of the Arnhem bridge. Here, with most of his battalion, plus some of brigade headquarters, less the brigade commander, he held on against fierce attacks, until overrun. SS panzer grenadiers offered the survivors chocolate and brandy, congratulating them on the way they had fought.*

TOP Privates Jury and Malcolm man a Bren gun in the perimeter around Oosterbeek on 23 September. One of the many photographs taken by Sergeant Lewis.

ABOVE Corporal Tierney of the 1st Border Regiment and his three-inch mortar crew at Oosterbeek.

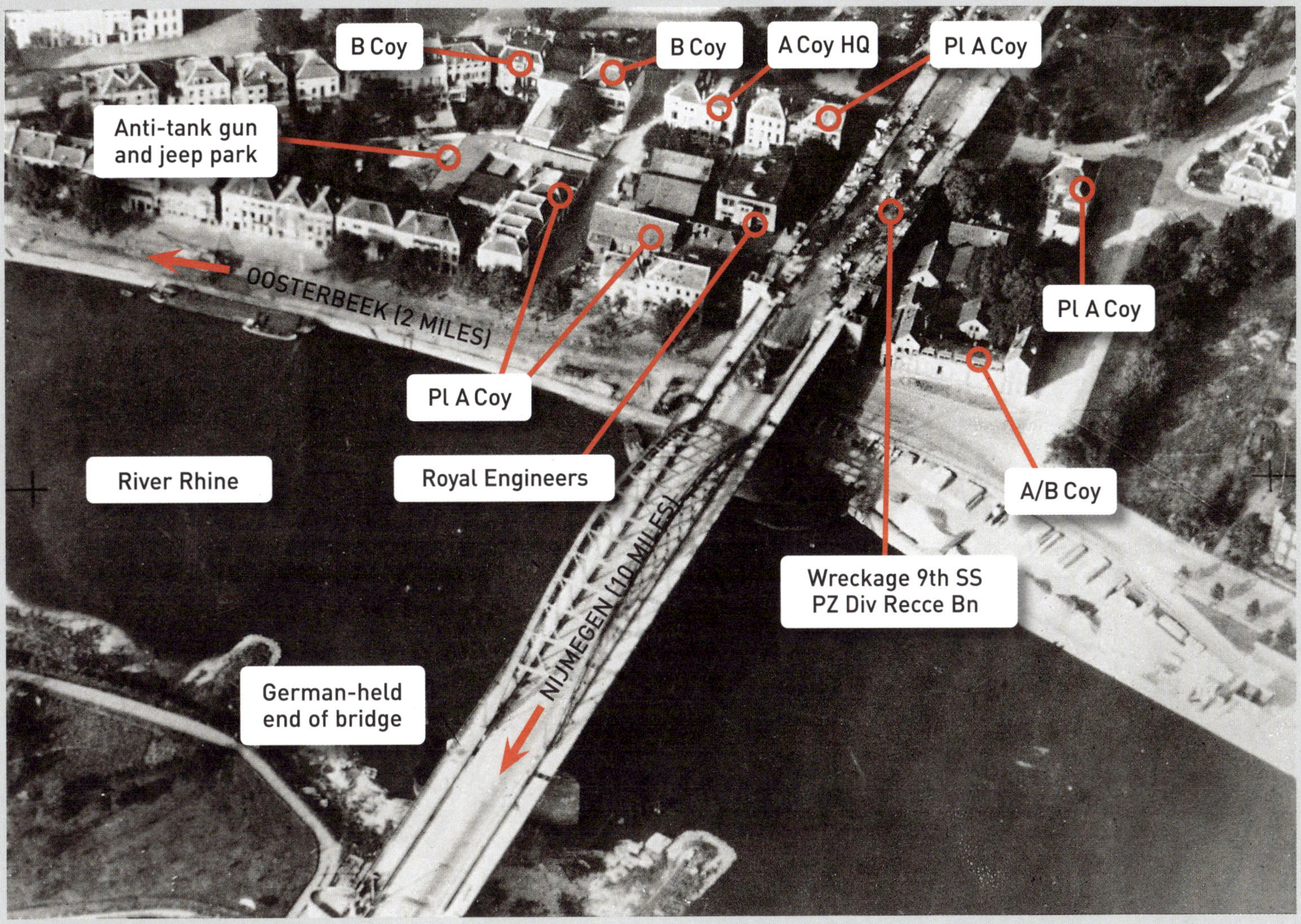

ABOVE Spitfire reconnaissance photo taken on the afternoon of 18 September 1944. Annotations show some of the company (Coy) and platoon (Pl) dispositions of 1 Parachute Group Force under command of Lieutenant Colonel John Frost.

LEFT British 1st Airborne Division badge.

The 1st and 3rd Battalions ran into heavy opposition and eventually halted for the night. The following day all the efforts by these two battalions to join Frost at the bridge were repulsed with heavy losses. At the bridge, Frost's men held on grimly against repeated attacks supported by armour.

Meanwhile the 1st Air Landing Brigade, which had also arrived on the first day, was holding the drop zone for the arrival of the 4th Parachute Brigade on Monday 18 September. Urquhart, unable to find out what was happening because the radios were not working, had gone forward on the first day, and was cut off in the outskirts of Arnhem with the badly wounded Lathbury.

The 4th Parachute Brigade suffered a number of casualties on the drop from the thoroughly alerted enemy. The Brigade's move into Arnhem on the northern route was stopped in its tracks with heavy casualties. As they withdrew, the Germans followed up. After a desperate battle fought with great gallantry, the remnants of the Brigade managed to escape the clutches of the enemy. Eventually Urquhart rejoined his division, and it became clear that despite further superhuman efforts to reach Frost by the remnants of 1st, 3rd and 11th Parachute Battalions, and 2nd Battallion South Staffordshire Regiment, the German defences were too strong. In the ferocious fighting all commanding officers were killed or wounded. Urquhart ordered that a defensive perimeter be formed around the Hartenstein Hotel at Oosterbeek. The fighting at the bridge continued for the whole of the next day, and on until the morning of the following day. Frost was wounded in both legs. Ammunition ran out. Eventually

17–26 SEPTEMBER 1944

ARNHEM

KEY

Front line 17 September

Front line 21 September

Final perimeter 26 September

Parachute drop zone

Glider landing zone

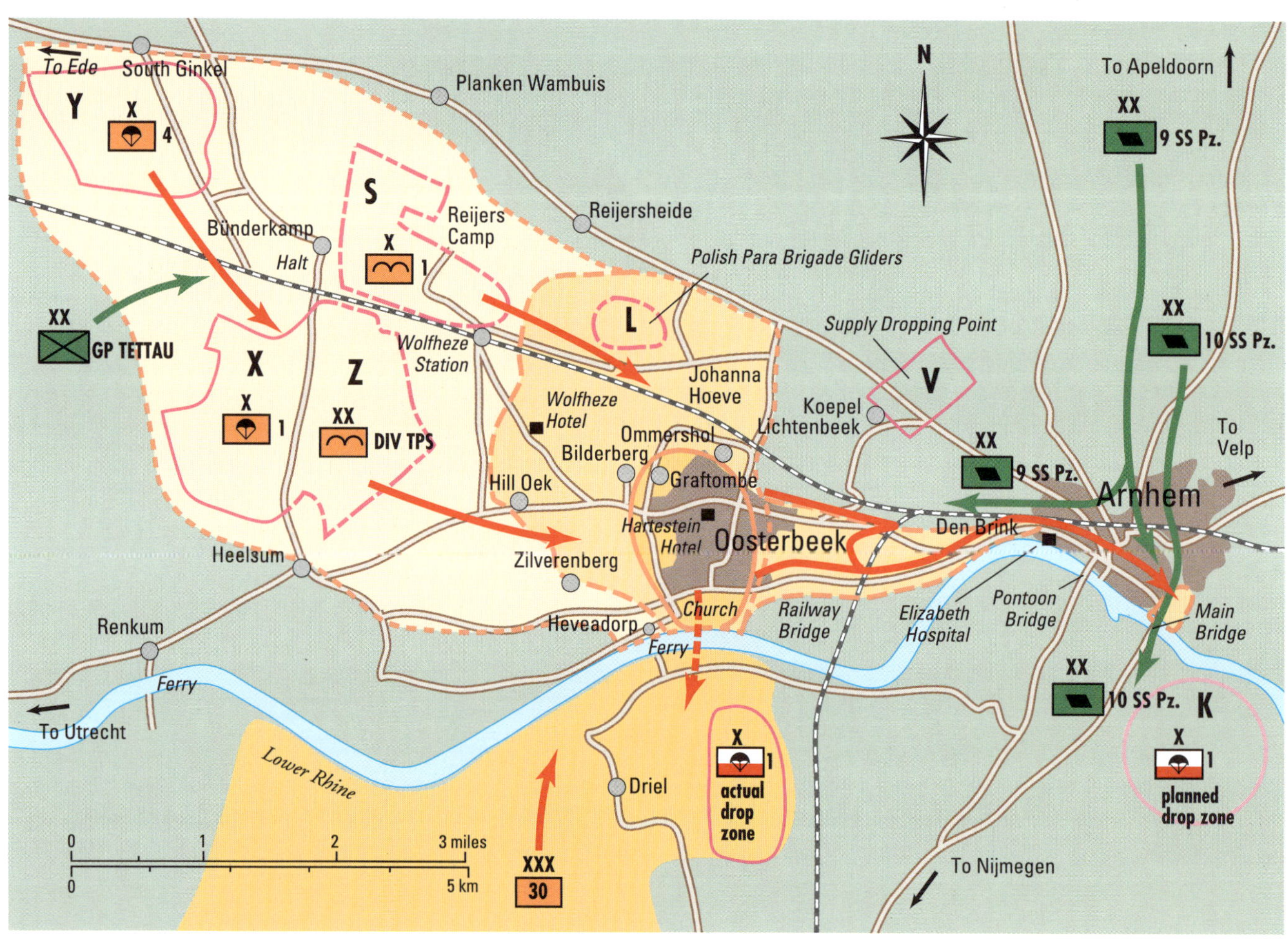

MAJOR ROBERT CAIN VC *found his B Company, 2nd Battalion South Staffordshire Regiment cut off during the Battle of Arnhem. During the ensuing six days he fought off repeated German attempts to break into his position near Oosterbeek church. With a Projectile, Infantry, Anti-Tank (PIAT) he single-handedly knocked out a Tiger tank, and later drove off three more in the same way. Throughout, although suffering from multiple wounds, he encouraged his men by his fearless example. His actions earned him the Victoria Cross (right).*

WAR CORRESPONDENTS *accompanied the troops throughout the campaign. Arnhem footage was taken by three parachuting Army Film Unit cameramen: Mike Lewis, Jock Walker and Dennis Smith. The BBC's Stanley Maxted and Guy Byam recorded their battle impressions on wax discs. Alan Wood (right) reported for the "Daily Express" and combined world press. Reuters was represented by Jack Smythe, and Marek Swiecicki reported on the Poles.*

the battalion was overrun at 09. 00 on Thursday morning. For the first time since Sunday night, the Germans could cross the bridge. The original Allied plan called for the complete division to hold it for 48 hours; in the event, a battalion held it for three days and four nights.

While the remnants of the division held out in Oosterbeek, Major General Stanislaw Sosabowski's Polish Parachute Brigade was dropped south of the Rhine near Driel. No boats were available and the Poles were unable to cross. Although XXX Corps managed to close up to the south bank of the Rhine by 22 September, only small parties of men managed to cross.

Eventually on the night of 25–26 September 2,183 men of the 1st Airborne Division, which had flown into battle 10,000 strong, were withdrawn over the Rhine. 1,400 were dead, and over 6,000 were prisoners including the wounded. Each parachute brigade consisted of less than a company, and the air-landing brigade consisted of less than a battalion.

ABOVE German photograph taken at about 3.00 p.m. on 21 September, near the Arnhem bridge. Left to right, Sapper Grier and Lance Corporal Robb of 1st Parachute Squadron Royal Engineers, shelled and burned out of the school they had occupied since the evening of 17 September.

RIGHT Detailed Dutch Resistance report on the strength of German forces in the Arnhem area. This report was ignored by the "Market Garden" planners. See translation on page 156.

13 en 14 September 1944. H.G.

Langs beide zijden van IJssel, tussen Zwolle en Arnhem en in Achterhoek is gelegerd en is nog bezig zich te legeren:
SS. Divisie Hohenstaufen.
Teken op auto's: geel schild, blauwe rand, waarin blauwe hoofdletter H en verticaal blauw zwaard.
Divisiestaf vermoedelijk in Doetinchem. Nog geen nadere gegevens.
Andere staven, vermoedelijk regimentsstaven, in Beekbergen en Epse.
Beekbergen: Stfkrt. 33. Zutphen W., uitg. '34.
a. 13.65-63.95: Hotel.
Borden: IV A.R. Halt. Abt. II[a] en II[b].
b. 14,1 -63,7 : Abt. IV[b] Skalke Jäger.
c. 14,3 -63,87: Postkantoor, Rode vlag met witte F.
d. 14,25-63,9 : Rode vlag met witte F.bliksemschicht.
Verder. I/20; VI; SS Jense en nog 4 eenheden.
Totaal in Beekbergen: ong. 300 man SS. wit en rood.
Epse: Café "De Pessink" (wegsplitsing Deventer-Zutphen, Deventer-Lochem): Rode vlag met witte F. ong. 100 SS. rood.
Deventer: ong. 50 SS wit.
Diepenveen: ong. 500 SS wit. zag: 3 pantserwagens, lagn 4,5 M. hoog 1.50 M., bewapend met zware m.g. of pak.
zag: 8 stuk pak (6 cm.).
Gorssel: ong. 250 SS rood.
Weg Apelddorn-Zutphen tussen De Kar en Empe.
ong. 300 SS rood, zag. 6 stuk pak (3,7 cm.)
Borden Grau; grau 2 en grau 3.
Klarenbeek: Hotel: Abt. IV[a] en Flak 10 Schraubs ong. 10 SS wit.
Loenen. Hotel Eikenboom: ong. 150 SS wit en rood.
Bord M rood
Vaassen. ongeveer 50 SS wit.
Apeldoorn. ongeveer 100 SS wit (Hohenstaufen) Borden I/19 en II/19
(bovendien oude SS bezettingong. 100 man).
Richting Hoenderlo: ong. 80 SS.
Arnhem: Meldekopf Hohenstaufen.
H.V.P. Hohenstaufen.
Sax en Weimarkazerne. Borden M I; H 1; zag auto SS met rose
Vermoedelijk in Hohenstaufens verband opgenomen:
ong. 100 W.H. rose met 1 tank(6 cm. kanon) en 20 lichte pantserwagens.
Hierop: 4 en Witter rose
In Arnhem, Velp en Oosterbeek: ong. 1500 SS (geel, rose, wit en rood).
Achterhoek: SS in Vorden en Doetinchem (Div. Stab?!!).
Totaal naar schatting waargenoemn: ong. 3500-4000 man SS.. Hohenstaufen.

Verdere berichten:
Arnhem, 14 September: Willemskazerne: O.K.W. Feldjäger. adelaar V
Totaal 400-500 man W.H. wit en lichtgroen.
Bovendien: Fliegerfelddivision.
zag auto W.L. groen.
Oosterbeek-Wolfheze 14 Sept. ong. 750 WH. rood, ong. 30 stuk 10 cm.veld
Epse 13 September: Nog aanwezig 2500 vaten à 200 L. benzine. rood
Apeldoorn.13 September:
Airforce: Willem III kazerne: Luisterapparaten worden verwijderd.
Huidige bezetting:
A.F. 25 W.L. bruin; 50 W.L. rood(o.a. O.K.W. Panzerjäger)
Army: 100 WH blauw
100 Grüne Pol.
Defensie: Emplacement 4 stuk vierling Flak 2 cm.
Zutphen 13 September:

RIGHT Original typed and hand-amended copy of one of war correspondent Alan Wood's reports on the desperate battle in Arnhem. The ink writing at the bottom of the page is a "passed for publication" confirmation by the Allied Expeditionary Force censor.

PRD E SHAEF MINIFORM LONDON XX FOR COMBINED BRITISH PRESS FROM ALAN WOOD

Censored by Brett 26

With Allied airborne forces Arnhem area Friday 9 a.m.

Its been a nasty morning so far cold and misty and the Germans are plastering us plentifully with mortars, big guns and 88s. The 88s are worst because you dont hear them coming. Machine guns have just opened up on the right.

In this patch of hell our men are holding a few civilian houses still stand. An old lady in black stumbled out of one of them a few minutes ago, and a British soldier ran out and put his arm round her. She collapsed and he carried her down to safety in a cellar.

It is now just five days and five sleepless nights since we flew out from England. God knows from what secret source of strenght these fighting men have drawn the guts which has kept them going. Only one thing is certain. They will keep going until the Second Army gets here.

More and more Second Army guns are firing in our support. They called the Brigadier at midnight and told him they were just going to fire another shoot. Good, he said, Ill stay up another ten minutes to see it.

Signalman Philip Timbrell of Birmingham is sitting beside me shouting quote down sir unquote dash rather as if I were a dog dash when he hears a shell coming. I asked him if he had any message he wanted sent back. Quote tell them its my birthday unquote he says stop he is 23

end

Passed for publication
Brett 26
AEF Censor

CLEARING THE SCHELDT ESTUARY

TUESDAY 3 OCTOBER–SUNDAY 26 NOVEMBER 1944

The port of Antwerp, captured intact in early September, lay idle, its seaward access held by the Germans. Until Antwerp could be used, the Allied advance would stall for lack of supplies. Monty, belatedly, gave the opening of the Scheldt "complete priority over all other operations". By the end of October, Canadian, Polish, and British troops of Lieutenant General Guy Simonds' II Canadian Corps, had closed up to the River Maas and cleared both banks of the Scheldt estuary, including the Breskens Pocket and South Beveland. The fighting in the flooded polder was savage and exhausting – Allied efforts were greatly assisted by Hobart's specialized armour, now including the tracked amphibian the "Buffalo".

ABOVE The gap in the dyke at Westkapelle, Walcheren Island, shortly after bombing by Lancasters. The sea pours in to flood the interior of the island.

"Complete priority over all other offensive operations"

21ST ARMY GROUP DIRECTIVE, 9 OCTOBER 1944, REFERRING TO OPENING THE SCHELDT ESTUARY.

With the sides of the sea corridor held by the Allies, all that remained was to force the "door", and sweep the waterway clear of mines. The "door" was Walcheren, a saucer-shaped island, whose rim consisted of high sandy dunes. The Westkapelle dyke filled a gap in the dunes on the western edge. German batteries were built into the dunes in massive concrete emplacements, protected by minefields.

Simonds ordered the Westkapelle dyke to be breached by bombing. Foreseeing that the Germans would partially flood the "saucer" to make the attacker's job more difficult, his brilliant idea was to go the full stretch and flood it completely. The Allies, with amphibious vehicles, could penetrate the gap in the dyke, and use the floodwater for mobility inside the "saucer", in places attacking positions from the rear.

A three-pronged attack followed. From the east the 52nd (Lowland) Division attacked across the Walcheren-South Beveland causeway. No 4 Commando assaulted Flushing across the estuary from Breskens in Landing Craft Assaults (LCAs). Brigadier Leicester's 4th Commando Brigade (41, 47 and 48 Royal Marines Commandos) assaulted Westkapelle two hours after dawn on 1 November 1944, preceded by bombing and bombardment from the sea.

As the landing craft carrying Leicester's brigade ran in towards Westkapelle, it became clear that the bombing and shelling had not silenced the German batteries north and south of the gap in the dyke. Landing Craft Guns (LCGs), also manned by Royal Marines, closed

"It had been a hard and bloody business."

CANADIAN OFFICIAL HISTORIAN

ABOVE Canadian and British troops being briefed by an Armoured Corps officer (wearing a black beret) for operations on the Beveland Peninsula, before boarding their Buffalos.

LEFT Canadian II Corps badge.

to engage the batteries at point-blank range in support of their Marine comrades in the three commandos. Of the 25 LCGs only four remained fit for action. Their self-sacrifice, which drew the fire of the batteries, was not in vain. Casualties among the first two waves of landing craft and commandos were light. But without the fire of the LCGs to distract them, the batteries took a heavy toll of follow-up waves, many landing craft and buffalos were hit, and the commandos had to swim ashore.

ABOVE First used by the British at Walcheren, the American-designed Buffalo, fully amphibious and propelled by its tracks in the water, carried up to 30 troops, or a jeep or Universal Carrier. It had a crew of four and weighed 15 tons.

LIEUTENANT GENERAL GUY SIMONDS *was a junior staff officer in 1939, and commanded the Canadian 1st Infantry Division in Sicily and 5th Armoured in Italy. Highly regarded by Monty, Simonds led the Canadian I Corps from Normandy to the end of the war, except during the 85-day battle for the Scheldt Estuary, when he commanded Canadian First Army during Crerar's absence on sick leave. He was an innovative tactician, using searchlights reflected on clouds to produce artificial moonlight, and devised the first armoured personnel carriers.*

Once ashore, the fighting was bitter and prolonged. The commandos cleared the concrete casemates and gun positions, ploughing through deep sand, and losing men on mines as they closed with the enemy. 47 Commando lost all five rifle troop commanders in one hour, clearing the final battery between Westkapelle and Flushing. Mopping up on Walcheren ended on 8 November.

Minesweeping the estuary started before Walcheren had been cleared. The port of Antwerp was opened on 26 November, completely transforming the supply position of the Allied armies.

ABOVE After being hit several times, the crew of an LCG (Landing Craft Gun) abandons the craft.

LEFT British Commando badge.

ABOVE A Landing Craft Tank (LCT) discharges Buffalos to swim ashore at Westkapelle; one has landed, visible far left of this picture.

ABOVE Buffalos and a bulldozer come ashore from a beached LCT in a sea of mud and among beach obstacles, some of which were mined.

3 OCTOBER–26 NOVEMBER 1944

THE SCHELDT ESTUARY

KEY

- Front line 1 October
- Front line 27 October
- Front line 8 November
- Flooded area

AACHEN AND HURTGEN FOREST

WEDNESDAY 13 SEPTEMBER–SATURDAY 9 DECEMBER 1944

Aachen could have been taken in mid September. When Lieutenant General Courtney Hodges's US First Army entered Germany, General Count Gerhard von Schwerin, deeming that the war was lost and wishing to avoid unnecessary destruction, declared Aachen an open city. Unaware that Aachen lay undefended, Major General Joseph "Lightning Joe" Collins's VII Corps bypassed the city aiming to breach the Siegfried Line, or Westwall, before the Germans could gather themselves after their headlong retreat. Having achieved a shallow penetration, and short of fuel, his advance petered out in the face of an infantry division that Hitler had personally deployed from East Prussia. Aachen was special: Charlemagne, in Nazi mythology the founder of the First Reich, was buried there. The whole of Hodges's Army, overextended by the dash from the Seine, ground to a halt.

After the failure of Market Garden, Eisenhower directed that Bradley would advance to the Rhine with US First and Ninth Armies. First, Hodges had to take Aachen. His soldiers battled slowly through the defences of the Westwall north of Aachen, eventually linked up with the salient previously achieved by "Lightning Joe" Collins, and surrounded the city. After bitter house-to-house fighting, Aachen surrendered on 21 October – the first German city to fall to the Allies.

On 2 November, the US 28th Division attacked a dense forest south-east of Aachen, making for high ground near Schmidt on which to anchor First Army's right flank for the breach of the Westwall. Ten days later the shattered division reeled back.

Neither Bradley nor Hodges appreciated the importance of two dams controlling the flow of water in the River Roer that ran through a low-lying plain that the First and Ninth Armies would have to cross on their way to the Rhine. The dams were overlooked by the 28th Division's objective. Naturally the Germans bitterly contested this key ground, inflicting over 6,000 casualties on the 28th Division, one of the war's mostly costly divisional attacks. The name of the forest

AACHEN AND HURTGEN CASUALTIES

ALLIED

US: 57,000 battle casualties (dead, wounded, missing)

70,000 Illness/frost-bite/fatigue

AXIS

50,000 battle casualties (estimate)

72,000 POWs

ABOVE US 28th Infantry Division badge.

LIEUTENANT GENERAL COURTNEY HODGES *joined the US Army as a private in 1906, and rose to rank of Lieutenant Colonel in the First World War, being decorated twice for gallantry. From being Bradley's deputy in US First Army, he moved up to command it when Bradley became an Army Group Commander.*

Underneath a quiet, unflappable exterior, Hodges was tough and resolute, nowhere more so than at the Battle of the Bulge where he successfully defied Montgomery's instructions on the timing of his counter-attack.

LIEUTENANT BERNARD J. RAY *was a platoon leader with Company F, 8th Infantry in the Hürtgen Forest. His company was halted by concertina wire. Under heavy fire he dashed forward, placed a torpedo under the wire and while connecting it to a charge he carried, was severely wounded by a mortar shell. With primer cord still wound about his body and explosive caps in his pocket, he completed a wiring system and thrust down on the handle of the charger, destroying himself along with the wire. By sacrificing his life, Lieutenant Ray enabled his company to continue its attack. He was posthumously awarded the Medal of Honor (right).*

would soon be heard with foreboding by thousands of American soldiers: Hürtgen.

The main offensive kicked off on 16 November after the war's heaviest air bombardment in support of ground troops. Its effect was disappointing, partly because in an effort to avoid friendly fire there was too great a distance between attacking troops and the bomb line. The fighting that followed was some of the most punishing of the war, in sleet, floods, mud, pillboxes, and worst of all the Hürtgen Forest, an evergreen jungle with shell-blasted trees like a scene from *Grimm's Fairy Tales*.

Hoping that one more attack might break the Germans, Hodges fed his divisions into the forest meat grinder one by one, disregarding the reality that so long as the Roer dams remained in enemy hands, no Americans could cross the Roer. Had these dams been seized first by a full-blooded attack, the Germans would have been forced to withdraw, or would have been cut off.

By 9 December most of the Hürtgen was cleared at a cost of over 29,000 American casualties, including 5,000 cases of trench foot and battle shock. Eight divisions had been mangled in the forest. The fighting here died down, flaring up again after the Battle of the Bulge. The forest was not completely cleared until 3 February 1945. To the north, First and Ninth Armies closed up to the banks of the Roer, losing 57,000 battle casualties, and another 70,000 to exposure, disease and fatigue. The First Army alone lost 550 tanks, enough to equip two armoured divisions.

Despite the agony, the Americans had not reached the Rhine; they were still stuck on the Roer.

ABOVE Jagd (hunting) Panther, a self-propelled anti-tank gun, with a fixed turret, and 88mm gun. Often the vehicle had to be swung to aim the gun, so it was not popular with crews from proper tanks.

"We had the bear by the tail, and we just couldn't turn loose."

GENERAL THORSON, CHIEF OF OPERATIONS, US FIRST ARMY

ABOVE Private Zukerbrow takes cover behind a disabled German 47mm anti-tank gun during street fighting in Aachen.

ABOVE Fighting in the Hürtgen Forest. This was one of the most costly US battles of the Second World War.

12 SEPTEMBER–9 NOVEMBER 1944

AACHEN AND HURTGEN FOREST

KEY
- Front line 12 September
- Front line 18 September
- Siegfried Line (Westwall)
- Front line 16 October
- Front line 9 November

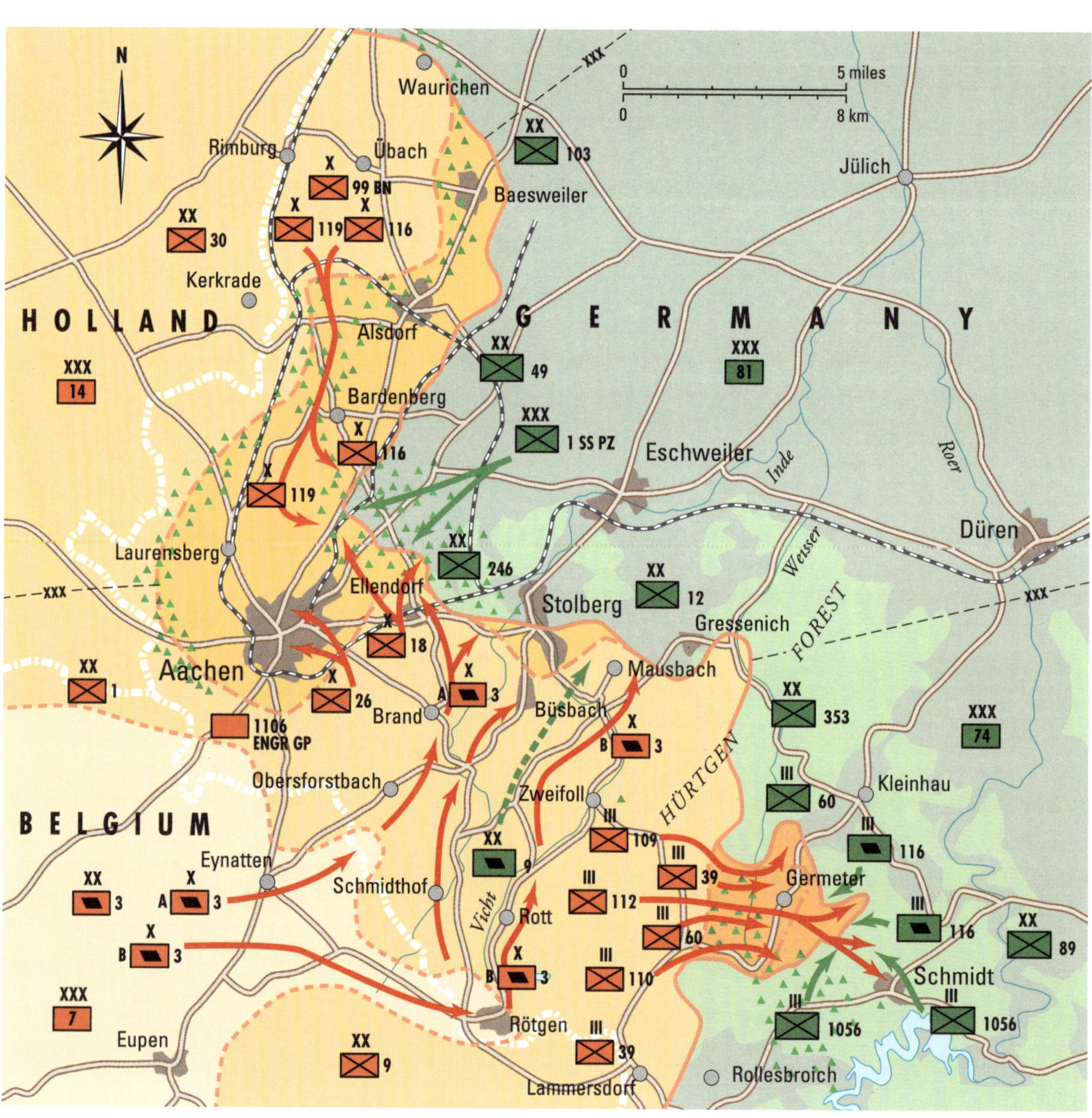

RIGHT *My Military Missal* issued by the National Catholic Community Service for use by all branches of the US Armed Forces.

MY
MILITARY
MISSAL

EDITED BY
FATHER STEDMAN
FOR ALL BRANCHES
OF THE ARMED FORCES

MASS FOR THE DEAD

† This cross in margin of Ordinary (pages 7, 8, 12, 13, 15, 21, 38, 44), indicates paragraph is omitted in Mass for Dead. (*Use this Mass on All Souls Day, November 2nd*).

PICTURE AND MASS THEME EXPLAINED

May *"those whom the certainty of dying afflicts, be consoled by the promise of future immortality."*

The scales of life and eternity! All present things must be measured by our future glory (Palms and crown of victory in the middle). *"An eternal dwelling is being prepared in heaven"* for those who live by faith, hope and charity (symbols on the left); who ever behold *"the abode of this earthly sojourn being dissolved"* one day, symbolized at right by the toppling castles of earthly dreams.

NOW BEGIN MASS AT 1 ON PAGE 7.

ETERNAL REST give to them, O Lord; INTROIT Ps. 64 2

68

MY MILITARY MISSAL 69

and let perpetual light shine upon them.† A hymn, O God, becometh Thee in Sion; and a vow shall be paid to Thee in Jerusalem: O Lord, hear my prayer; all flesh shall come to Thee. Eternal rest, etc.

Turn to 3 on page 11.

O GOD, the bestower of pardon PRAYERS 4 and lover of man's salvation, we beseech Thy Clemency, through the intercession of Blessed Mary, ever a Virgin, and all Thy Saints, so that the brethren of our congregation, our relatives and benefactors who have passed out of this world, may together enjoy everlasting happiness. Through our Lord Jesus Christ, Thy Son, Who lives and reigns with Thee in the unity of the Holy Spirit, God, world without end. [R] Amen. ↓ *Continue below.*

O GOD, Who art ever inclined to pity and to spare, have mercy on the souls of Thy servants and handmaids, and forgive them all their sins, so that after their departure from this life, they may enter life eternal.

Continue on next page.

PATTON'S PROGRESS

THURSDAY 31 AUGUST–WEDNESDAY 13 DECEMBER 1944

Patton's Third Army rolled into Lorraine at the end of August, led by Major General Walton Walker's XX Corps heading for Metz in the north, and the XII Corps in the south aimed at Nancy. Eisenhower kept Patton on a tight rein until mid-September to preserve supplies for Montgomery's offensive in the north, so that although Nancy was soon taken, the fortress of Metz remained in enemy hands. A ring of 35 forts defended the city. The key was Fort Driant, a complex of forts in itself, guarding the southern approaches. Patton confidently said to Walker, "see you in Metz".

Patton had fought in Lorraine in the First World War and should have known better than to mount head-on attacks in such terrain. In his self-imposed mission to win the war single-handed, he ignored the fact that the heady days of pursuit against a beaten foe were over. The weather was appalling, heavy rain flooded the rivers and the ground was a sea of mud.

Patton wanted Metz as a trophy to present to General George C. Marshall, the US Army Chief-of-Staff, when he visited Third Army, and ordered Walker to take the city regardless of casualties. The assault failed bloodily, and even Patton began to recognize that Metz might cost much more blood than he was prepared to spill. Walker, with the bit between his teeth, pressed on until two of his divisional commanders refused to continue with the attacks. Patton supported them, and ordered Walker to call off further attacks for the time being.

ABOVE US 95th Infantry Division badge.

BELOW AND BELOW RIGHT Infantry of Patton's Third Army advance into the outskirts of the fortress town of Metz, the last German stronghold in France.

"We roll across France in less time than it takes Monty to say 'regroup' and here we sit stuck in the mud of Lorraine."

PATTON

ABOVE On their way to Metz, infantry advance through vineyards to the Moselle River under cover of smoke.

LIEUTENANT GENERAL GEORGE PATTON *was a dedicated and highly professional soldier who commanded a tank brigade in the First World War. He took over US II Corps in Tunisia in 1942 when its commander was sacked. While commanding US Seventh Army in Sicily, he slapped two battle-shocked soldiers. Eisenhower saved him from dismissal, and instead he commanded the US Third Army in a series of brilliant operations in north-west Europe. Feared by German generals for his unpredictability, his counter-attack in the Bulge was his highlight.*

Patton complained about the weather, the lack of supplies, Monty and Eisenhower, taking out his frustration on his staff, and even on his beloved bull terrier Willie. He dreamed of taking Fort Driant as a 59th birthday present to himself, but instead fell into the trap for which he castigated others, ordering piecemeal attacks that played into the hands of the German defenders and failed.

Metz eventually fell to the 95th Division (the "Iron men of Metz") on 22 November, after heavy close-quarter fighting to winkle out the German defenders from every room, strongpoint and tunnel. The commander of Army Group G, General Hermann Balck, was scathing about Patton, remarking that the motley collection of German troops were badly equipped, but defended Metz so successfully thanks entirely to the bad leadership of the Americans.

Although Patton swept into Metz with much publicity and self-congratulation, Fort Driant and other smaller forts held out for another three weeks, their garrisons surrendering on 13 December, only when their food ran out.

LIEUTENANT GENERAL WALTON WALKER

LIEUTENANT GENERAL WALTON WALKER *who commanded XX Corps in Patton's Third Army, was nicknamed "Bulldog" both for his appearance and for his fighting disposition. Patton sometimes called him "fat Walker", but more often "a fighting son of a bitch". Walker had a tendency to sack his divisional commanders the first time they made a mistake, and on at least two occasions Patton had to overrule him. A thrusting general like Patton whom he idolized, he would push armour through terrain thought to be impossible for tanks.*

LEFT Armour and infantry moving along muddy roads and past bleak winter trees towards the centre of Metz.

BELOW LEFT Soldiers of Patton's Third Army examining the reinforced concrete defences of Fort Driant, one in the ring of forts outside Metz.

BELOW Artillery of Patton's Third Army battling with the mud outside Metz. The mud was reminiscent of the First World War, as was some of the fighting.

ABOVE US XX Corps badge.

3 SEPTEMBER–15 DECEMBER 1944

PATTON'S PROGRESS

KEY

Front line 3 September
Front line 14 September
Front line 8 November
Front line 15 December

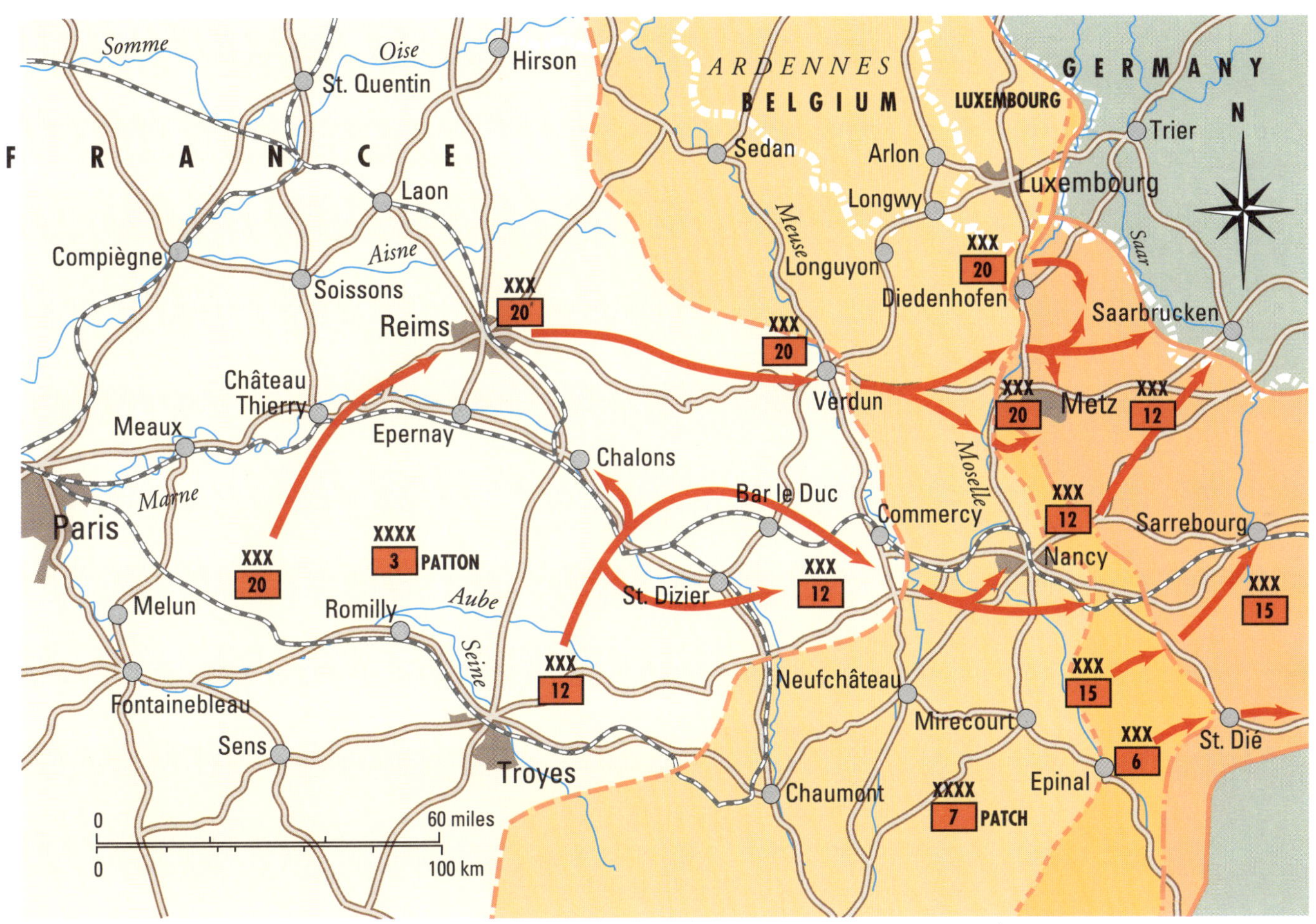

BELOW Montgomery's handwritten telegram of 21 September to Eisenhower putting his case in the strongest terms for priority of supplies for his 21st Army Group in the north, over the needs of Bradley's 12th Army Group to Montgomery's right. Where he says, "the right flank of 12th Army Group should be given a very direct order to halt," he is referring to Patton's Third Army.

M 526 Most Immediate

SHAEF FWD

M 223 ⊙ TOPSEC ⊙ Personal and EYES ONLY for Eisenhower from Montgomery ⊙ Dear IKE ⊙ Thank you very much for your letter of 20 Sep sent via GALE ⊙ I cannot agree that our concepts are the same and I am sure you would wish me to be quite frank and open in the matter ⊙ I have always said stop the right and go on with the left but the right has been allowed to go on so far that it has outstripped its maintenance and we have lost flexibility ⊙ in your letter you still want to go on further with your right and you state in your para 6 that ALL of BRADLEYS Army Group will move forward sufficiently etc ⊙ I would say that the right flank of 12 Army Group should be given a very direct order to halt and if this order is not obeyed we shall get into greater difficulties ⊙ the nett result of the matter in my opinion is that if you want to get the RUHR you will have to put every single thing into the left hook and stop everything else ⊙ it is my opinion that if this is NOT done then you will NOT get the RUHR ⊙ your very great friend MONTY ⊙

B.L.M.
1955 hrs
21-9-44

RIGHT Patton's letter to Major General Scott, who commanded the Armored Center back in the States, reveals a thoughtful side to Patton – very different from the popular image of a profane, "blood and guts" general who cared little for his men.

HEADQUARTERS
THIRD UNITED STATES ARMY
OFFICE OF THE COMMANDING GENERAL
APO 403

29 September, 1944

My dear Scotty:

Thanks very much for your letter. I should think from the description that the T-33 is just what we need.

The other day, Colonel Clark, who commands Combat Command "A" of the 4th Armored Division, and whom you will remember as Engineer of the 7th Cavalry Brigade, attacked TROYES with one medium tank company in line backed up by two companies of infantry in carriers. They advanced, all guns firing, for 5,000 meters across open country, killed 600 Germans and took the town without a casualty to man or machine. The carrier you described would be good for this.

Clark also says, and I agree with him, that the co-axial machine gun in our tanks is the most deadly weapon we have. His Combat Command has captured and destroyed twenty-nine 88's by shooting the crews away from them with this weapon. He believes, and I do too, that it would be a great improvement if an additional co-axial, preferably a .50, but failing that a .30, could be placed in all our tanks. Anything you can do in this matter will be appreciated. If it is feasible, let me know and I will write Somervell to push it.

With affectionate regards to Helen, I am as ever,

Devotedly yours,

G. S. PATTON, JR.

Major General C. L. Scott
Headquarters Armored Center
Fort Knox, Kentucky
U. S. A.

BATTLE OF THE BULGE: ONSLAUGHT

SATURDAY 16 DECEMBER–SUNDAY 17 DECEMBER 1944

At 5.30 a.m. on 16 December 1944, 13 infantry and seven German armoured divisions, with 970 tanks and assault guns and another 450 in reserve, were poised to attack the Americans in Belgium on a 60-mile front between Monschau and Echternach. Another five divisions would join them soon. This attack was Hitler's brainchild. Although the toadies in his headquarters, including Field Marshal Wilhelm Keitel, supported Hitler, many senior German commanders were appalled when they were briefed on the plan – Operation *Wacht am Rhein*. They recognized that Hitler risked frittering away reserves that would be needed for the forthcoming battle in Germany.

Three German armies had been assembled in conditions of utmost secrecy. The sentence of death awaited any German who so much as breathed a word about what was to come. Only Hitler, his personal staff, Field Marshal Gerd von Rundstedt Commander-in-Chief West, and Model commanding Army Group B, with four staff officers from

BATTLE OF THE BULGE

AXIS

THREE ARMIES:
Sixth Panzer: Sepp Dietrich
Fifth Panzer: Hasso von Manteuffel
Seventh: Erich Brandenberger

ASSAULT DIVISIONS:
13 infantry divisions
8 armoured divisions
In Reserve: 5 divisions

ALLIES

US VIII CORPS:
Lt Gen Troy Middleton
5 divisions

ABOVE A German soldier photographed during the Battle of the Bulge.

FIELD MARSHAL GERD VON RUNDSTEDT *was a Prussian aristocrat whose First World War record gained him high command in the Second. Promoted to Field Marshal in July 1940, his adherence to the Prussian code of military honour made him incapable of opposing Hitler and his regime. But he never feared to argue with Hitler, who respected him enough to bring him back from retirement twice as Commander-in-Chief West. He was finally sacked after the US capture of the Remagen Bridge on 7 March 1945.*

ABOVE German soldiers from 9th Parachute Regiment, 3rd Parachute Division strip dead American soldiers of their boots in Honsfeld after being attached to Peiper's Battle Group for the break-in battle.

BELOW A film still from a recreation of an engagement between 1st SS Panzer Division and a convoy of 14th US Cavalry Group. Shot almost immediately after the action, it shows 7th Armored Division's Combat Command A near a crossroads on the exit road from St Vith.

each of their headquarters were party to the plan until just before the jump-off day. From north to south the German deployment was Sixth Panzer Army (General Sepp Dietrich), Fifth Panzer Army (General Hasso von Manteuffel), and the mainly infantry Seventh Army (General Erich Brandenberger). The two panzer armies were to slice forward towards Antwerp, while Seventh Army protected their flank against counter-attack by Patton's Third Army in the south. With Antwerp in German hands, Hitler hoped the Allies would sue for peace.

Hitler hoped to split the Allies apart, and repeat Dunkirk. The offensive bore many of the hallmarks of the stunning German breakthrough at Sedan in 1940 through much the same area, and

16–25 DECEMBER 1944

BATTLE OF THE BULGE

KEY

Front line 16 December
Front line 20 December
Front line 25 December
DZ Parachute drop zone

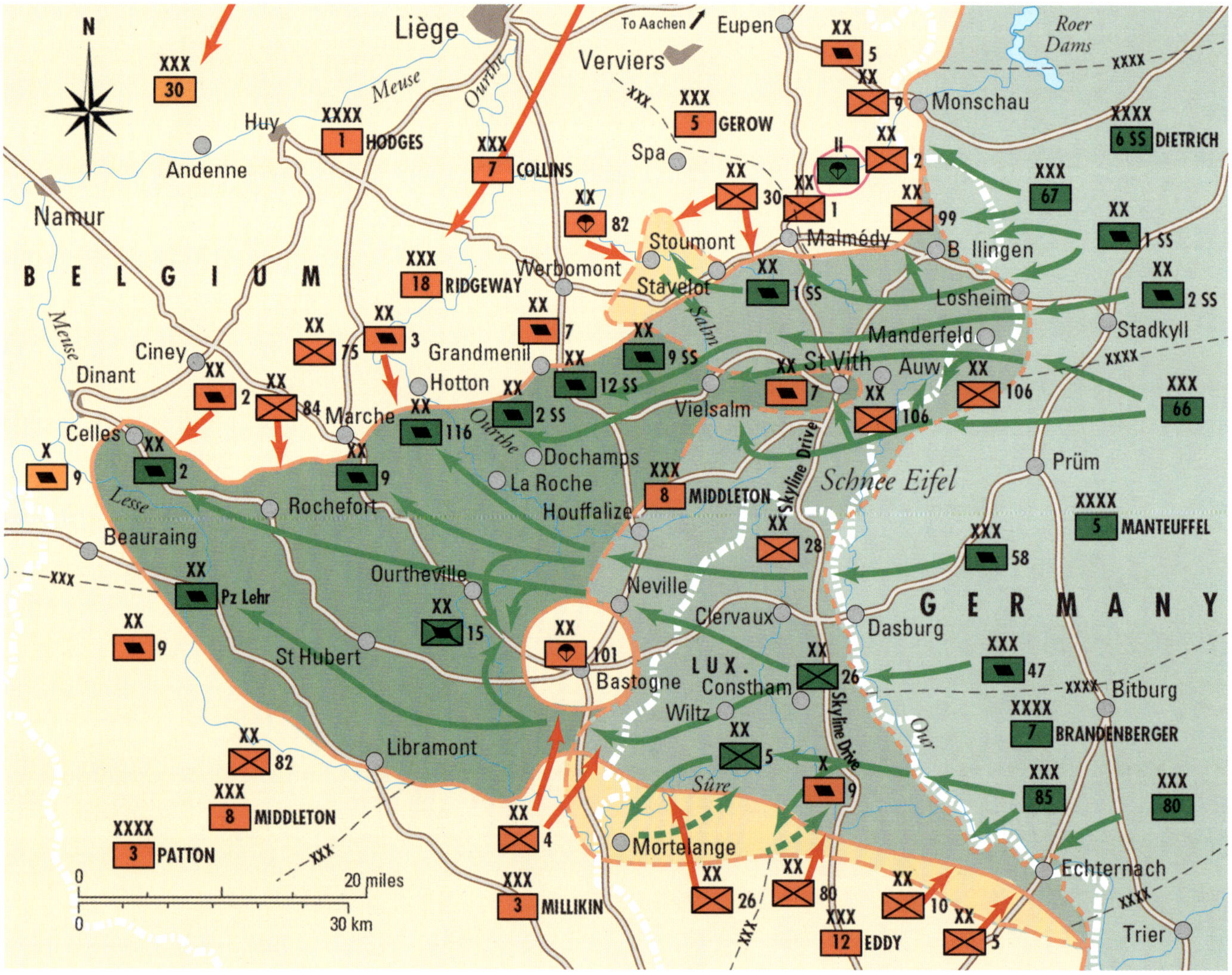

N
Liège
To Aachen
Eupen
Roer Dams
Verviers
Meuse
Ourthe
Huy
Andenne
Namur
Spa
Monschau
Stoumont
Malmédy
Büllingen
Werbomont
Stavelot
Salm
Losheim
Stadkyll
Manderfeld
St Vith
Auw
Grandmenil
Hotton
Vielsalm
Marche
Ciney
Dinant
Celles
Dochamps
La Roche
Houffalize
Schnee Eifel
Skyline Drive
Prüm
Rochefort
Lesse
Beauraing
Ourtheville
Neville
Clervaux
Dasburg
St Hubert
Bastogne
LUX.
Constham
Wiltz
Bitburg
Our
Libramont
Sûre
Mortelange
Echternach
Trier
BELGIUM
GERMANY
30 XXX
1 HODGES XXXX
7 COLLINS XXX
5 GEROW XXX
18 RIDGEWAY XXX
6 SS DIETRICH XXXX
67 XXX
66 XXX
5 MANTEUFFEL XXXX
58 XXX
47 XXX
7 BRANDENBERGER XXXX
85 XXX
80 XXX
8 MIDDLETON XXX
3 PATTON XXXX
3 MILLIKIN XXX
12 EDDY XXX
Pz Lehr
0 20 miles
0 30 km

ABOVE A film still from the recreation of the attack on the 14th US Cavalry Group, at the road junction near St Vith.

ABOVE Men of the US 99th Infantry Division are marched into captivity past a Tiger II Tank of the 501st SS Heavy Panzer Battalion of Peiper's Battle Group.

relied on the Allies harbouring the same misconceptions as then – that the poor roads and rugged forests were not suitable for armoured thrusts, and therefore needed to be only lightly defended. Speed was of the essence; to "bounce" the crossings of the River Meuse before the Allies could move to block them, Dietrich hoped to reach the river within 24 hours, or 48 at the most, and head for Antwerp. Manteuffel, having crossed the Meuse, was to head for Brussels and eventually Antwerp, guarding Dietrich's left flank. To reach the Meuse, the Germans had first to get through St Vith and Bastogne where the inadequate road networks converged.

To spread confusion ahead of the attacking armies, Hitler created a special brigade under SS Colonel Otto Skorzeny, operating in American uniforms, to capture bridges and sabotage headquarters. To deny American reinforcements using the road south from Aachen, the final, and only night-time German parachute operation of the war took place. Led by Crete veteran Lieutenant Colonel Frederich-August von der Heydte, 870 parachutists dropped in the early hours of 17 December. Only 300 arrived on the correct drop zone, nine miles south-west of Monschau. The drop achieved nothing other than diverting American troops to hunt the scattered parachutists. After six days, von der Heydte surrendered to the Americans.

Only five American divisions held the line, mostly new formations, or ones resting after a mauling in places like the Hürtgen Forest. Most of the front was the responsibility of Major General Troy Middleton's VIII Corps. Although taken by surprise, the Americans put up a stubborn resistance. Even when main bodies of units were overrun, small parties fought on grimly. The word soon got out that SS troops were massacring prisoners, providing good reason not to surrender. The inadequate roads, and narrow bridges over the steep-sided rivers were a further hindrance to swift progress, and soon both panzer armies were well behind their planned timetable.

SS COLONEL OTTO SKORZENY *was appointed to raise special commando units after a spell as Hitler's bodyguard, and serving in France and Russia in the Waffen SS. In September 1943 he snatched Mussolini from captivity at Gran Sasso d'Italia. For the Ardennes offensive, Hitler assigned him to lead Operation Greif (Snatch) behind American lines. Many of his men were caught and shot. After the war he founded Die Spinne (the Spider) that helped many of his SS comrades to escape from Germany.*

RIGHT Oberfahnrich Gunter Billing, a member of Skorzeny's Greif squads who operated in American uniforms, is tied to a stake before being shot near Herbestal.

BELOW A letter home by an excited Wehrmacht soldier of the 212th Volksgrenadier Division enjoying the brief fruits of victory in the initial German advance during the Battle of the Bulge. See translation on page 156.

Luxemburg, 21.12.44.

Liebe Paulstante!

3 Tage vor Weihnachten! Und wir sind am Vormarsch. Bis heute hatte ich so gar kein Weihnachtliches Gefühl! Erst heute hatten wir den ersten Schnee. Ich glaube, daß es Heuer nicht sehr arme Weihnachten werden bei uns hier. Denn der Amerikaner hinterlässt uns ganz nette und schöne Sachen. Sieh Dir zum Beispiel nur dieses Briefpapier an! Du machst Dir keine Vorstellung, was es hier noch alles gibt. Millionen von Bleistiften, tausende Strümpfe, Weine, Liköre, Marmelade, eingkochte Früchte, Zucker. Also Unmengen von jedem Gegenstand! So etwas muß man sehen sonst glaubt man es nicht. Alles liegt in den Geschäften am Boden und die Landser steigen mit den Dreckstiefel darauf 'rum und umwühlen das Ganze.

Hast Du die 100 RM. schon erhalten? — Sieh' es als kleines Weihnachtsgeschenk von mir an.

Herzliche Grüße

Karli.

BELOW An extremely rare set of "Happy Family" cards used for entertainment by German troops on the western front in the winter of 1944–45. Based on groups of German weapons and troop types, these four cards show the Heavy Infantry Weapon "family".

C.1. Schwere Infanterie-Waffen

Schweres Maschinengewehr

Die Schnellfeuerwaffe des Bataillons (M.G.K.)

2. Schwerer Granatwerfer
3. Infanterie-Geschütz
4. Pak, 3,7 cm

C.2. Schwere Infanterie-Waffen

Schwerer Granatwerfer

Die Steilfeuerwaffe des Bataillons

1. Schweres Maschinengewehr
3. Infanterie-Geschütz
4. Pak, 3,7 cm

C.3. Schwere Infanterie-Waffen

Infanterie-Geschütz

Das Begleitgeschütz des Infanterieangriffs

1. Schweres Maschinengewehr
2. Schwerer Granatwerfer
4. Pak, 3,7 cm

C.4. Schwere Infanterie-Waffen

Pak, 3,7 cm

Die Panzerabwehrwaffe des Regiments (14. Kp.)

1. Schweres Maschinengewehr
2. Schwerer Granatwerfer
3. Infanterie-Geschütz

BATTLE OF THE BULGE: CRISIS

MONDAY 18–FRIDAY 22 DECEMBER 1944

The stubborn defence by the Americans on the first days of the German offensive in the Ardennes, at such places as the Elsenborn Ridge, the Schnee Eifel, St Vith, the broad ridgeline bearing the road south of St Vith nicknamed by the Americans the "Skyline Drive", Clerf and the Sauer River Crossings, costly to both sides, imposed a drag on the German momentum. Fighting forward in existing positions, and wherever his troops encountered the enemy, rather than falling back, bought time for Middleton to re-deploy his meagre reserves. Even administrative troops; butchers and bakers, cooks and "bottlewashers", seized weapons and fought little actions that forced enemy columns to stop, deploy, put in an attack, expend precious time.

SS LIEUTENANT COLONEL JOCHEN PEIPER *served as Himmler's adjutant, and with 1st SS Panzer Division in Russia, Italy and France. In the Ardennes, his Kampfgruppe (KG – Battlegroup) Peiper, consisting of 4,800 men and over 800 vehicles, had the key role of spearheading the German advance on the north shoulder of the break-in. After making the best progress of any group, surrounded and out of fuel, KG Peiper was cut to pieces by US 30th Infantry Division and Combat Command B 3rd Armored.*

BELOW An American soldier runs past a burning half-track and weapons carrier that has received a direct hit from a German shell at Langlir, north-east of Houfflalize.

LEFT Often captioned as Lieutenant Colonel Jochen Peiper, the officer looking at the signpost is not Peiper but possibly one of his company commanders in a "Schwimmwagen", an amphibious jeep.

In their frustration, the Germans, and the SS in particular, sometimes shot prisoners. On their way to Stavelot, soldiers of Lieutenant Colonel Jochen Peiper's battlegroup massacred 19 prisoners while refuelling from captured stocks of American petrol. A little later, he encountered an American convoy near the town of Malmedy. While his main body pushed on, some of his battle group rounded up about 100 men from the convoy, marched them into a field, and amused themselves with a *"rabatz"*, an SS expression meaning to have fun killing everything in sight. Some Americans escaped by feigning death, but 86 died.

Full realization of the extent of the German successes filtered up the American chain of command very slowly, and to begin with was dismissed as a spoiling attack. Eventually, Eisenhower agreed to reinforce Hodges' First Army, including releasing the 82nd and 101st Airborne Divisions, withdrawn for a rest only three weeks previously after hard fighting in Holland after Market-Garden. The 82nd was sent to Werbomont, ten miles west of Stavelot, to block Peiper, who had passed through the village on his westward rampage.

The 101st, commanded by Brigadier General Anthony McAuliffe in General Maxwell Taylor's absence in the US, was ordered to hold the key road junction of Bastogne. The division was sent forward so quickly that some of their weapons were still in stores being refurbished. As the paratroopers marched up the road to Bastogne, they met soldiers from Middleton's Corps HQ ordered out of the town, whom they stopped, relieved of their weapons and ammunition, and pressed on.

RIGHT The Tiger II or King Tiger, a 70-ton tank with 150mm frontal armour, and an 88mm gun. Allied tanks found them difficult to destroy, and more were lost by mechanical failure than combat. Less than 500 were ever built.

BRIGADIER GENERAL ANTHONY C. McAULIFFE

commanded at Bastogne during Major General Maxwell Taylor's absence on leave in the USA. On 22 December, German emissaries under a flag of truce took a document in German to McAuliffe demanding the garrison's surrender. When told what it said, he laughed and said "Aw Nuts". Realizing a reply was required, he asked Colonel Harry Kinnard, his operations officer, what he should say, who suggested, "That first remark of yours would be hard to beat." "Nuts" was written on the paper.

If Manteuffel had seized Bastogne before the 101st's arrival, he would have been through to Dinant and Namur by 20 December. But the aggressive defence of the American paratroopers delayed and distracted three German divisions, who were unable to bypass the town. After failing to dislodge the 101st by direct assault, the Germans left a strong force to besiege the town, but although attacks drove in some of the outposts, the Germans could not penetrate the main defences. To a demand that the Americans surrender or be annihilated, McAuliffe's reply was "Nuts".

In the bitter cold, the magnificent 101st battled on with grim ardour. Some paratroopers used the frozen corpses of enemy soldiers to provide overhead cover on their foxholes. But help was on its way from Patton in the south.

"I just replied 'nuts', for I knew that one word best expressed the feelings of the division"

BRIGADIER GENERAL MCAULIFFE

ABOVE US 101st Airborne Division badge.

OPPOSITE TOP Soldiers of the 82nd Airborne Division plod through deep snow in the Ardennes, pulling their equipment on sleds and taking four exhausting days to cover just eight to 12 miles.

OPPOSITE BELOW 501st Parachute Infantry, 101st Airborne Division move up east of Bastogne on 19 December. They are liberally equipped with bazookas, and the leading man is carrying bazooka rockets.

TOP Bazooka gunner of 101st Airborne under an improvised shelter.

ABOVE A Sherman tank of the 4th Armored Division and a 30-calibre Browning machine gun crew guard the slim American corridor into Bastogne from the south.

RIGHT American soldiers hastily dig for protection while under enemy artillery fire near Berismenil. The soldier lying in the foreground has just been killed.

RIGHT Rare propaganda leaflet fired onto American frontline troops by German rifle grenade or propaganda rocket. It encourages the Americans to give themselves self-inflicted wounds so they can be home by Christmas. The recipient of this particular copy, during the Battle of the Bulge, has not taken up this suggestion, and on 23 December has written "Nazis in town 200 yards to our front".

MERRY

CHRISTMAS

Holidays! Well, they don't mean so much to me .... just sorta come and go. But now it's gettin on for Christmas, and being so far from home ... one kinda gets to thinkin of the folks, ... gee, ain't they far away. Ma and Pa and Sister Sue and lil' Benny ... gosh, all warm and cosy at home, 'n everything all smellin' of spice and cooking .... mince-meat pies ..... ummm.

Everybody hidin stuff and the old man always winkin in such a way to show he'd got sum'pin grand for Ma stuck away in the wood-shed. We all had sum'pin for Ma too ... and she'd a full sock for all of us. Golly, and came the 25th ... gee whiz, was that swell ... the tree n' all and everybody singin "Silent Night", n' "Hark the Herald Angels sing" ... and Ma so happy, she cried, like she always does ... Pa lookin so satisfied a' patting Ma on the back knowin he'd made her happy by cuttin down on the smokes to save up for that new dinner-service she'd always wanted. Boy-oh-boy, and the Christmas dinner ... Ma didn't have a turkey, she says their so dry ... pork-roast, cranberry sauce, mashed potatoes and gravy ... and MINCE-MEAT-PIE was the grandest yet. Gee, I wonder if it's the same this year, golly ... don't I wish I were there.

"Twas the night before Christmas
when all through the house
not a creature was stirring
not even a mouse!"

CHRISTMAS IN THE STATES?

.... WELL - WHY NOT?

Imagine if you should fall "ill".......

First Aid Station . . . . . . (on or about)		4th- 5th of Dec.
French War Hospital	,,	7th- 8th of Dec.
French Port	,,	9th-10th of Dec.
Departure from French Port with one of the "Christmas Steamers"	,,	12th-13th Dec.
Arrival in the States . . .	,,	19th-20th Dec.

CHRISTMAS IN U. S. HOSPITAL, or if you're lucky - AT HOME

Of course - in any case .... CONVALESCENCE FURLOUGH!

You think they may keep you back in France?

No danger! Every ill or slightly wounded man who is able to be transported will be sent home after the new regulations because the Hospitals in France must be left free for the seriously wounded of the now running large scale attack.

TAKE THE CHANCE - IT'S WORTH IT!

A.

RIGHT The only existing copy of General McAuliffe's famous "Merry Christmas" message sent at the crisis point of the Battle of the Bulge to all the men of the 101st Airborne Division surrounded in Bastogne. In it he recounts the story of his response to the German request to surrender: "NUTS!"

HEADQUARTERS 101ST AIRBORNE DIVISION
Office of the Division Commander

24 December 1944

What's Merry about all this, you ask? We're fighting - it's cold - we aren't home. All true but what has the proud Eagle Division accomplished with its worthy comrades of the 10th Armored Division, the 705th Tank Destroyer Battalion and all the rest? Just this: We have stopped cold everything that has been thrown at us from the North, East, South and West. We have identifications from four German Panzer Divisions, two German Infantry Division and one German Parachute Division. These units, spearheading the last desperate German lunge, were headed straight west for key points when the Eagle Division was hurriedly ordered to stem the advance. How effectively this was done will be written in history; not alone in our Division's glorious history but in World history. The Germans actually did surround us, their radios blared our doom. Their Commander demanded our surrender in the following impudent arrogance:

December 22nd 1944

"To the U. S. A. Commander of the encircled town of Bastogne.

The fortune of war is changing. This time the U. S. A. forces in and near Bastogne have been encircled by strong German Armored units. More German armored units have crossed the river Ourthe near Ortheuville, have taken Marche and reached St. Hubert by passing through Homores-Sibret-Tillet. Libramont is in German hands.

There is only one possibility to save the encircled U. S. A. Troops from total annihilation: that is the honorable surrender of the encircled town. In order to think it over a term of two hours will be granted beginning with the presentation of this note.

If this proposal should be rejected one German Artillery Corps and six heavy A. A. Battalions are ready to annihilate the U. S. A. Troops in and near Bastogne. The order for firing will be given immediately after this two hour's term.

All the serious civilian losses caused by this Artillery fire would not correspond with the well known American humanity.

The German Commander"

The German Commander received the following reply:

22 December 1944

"To the German Commander:

N U T S !

The American Commander"

Allied Troops are counterattacking in force. We continue to hold Bastogne. By holding Bastogne we assure the success of the Allied Armies. We know that our Division Commander, General Taylor, will say: "Well Done!"

We are giving our country and our loved ones at home a worthy Christmas present and being privileged to take part in this gallant feat of arms are trully making for ourselves a Merry Christmas.

/s/ A. C. McAULIFFE
/t/ A. C. McAULIFFE,
Commanding.

RIGHT The Friday 29 December 1944 edition of *Stars and Stripes*, the daily newspaper of the US Armed Forces, with first news of Patton's breakthrough to the surrounded defenders of Bastogne.

"We will remember you with pride and with humility. . . . We shall keep on remembering you." —*President Roosevelt.*

THE STARS AND STRIPES

Daily Newspaper of U.S. Armed Forces in the European Theater of Operations

". . . It is equally important that you complete the victory over Nazi ideas." —*Gen. Bradley.*

Vol. 1—No. 155 | 1 Fr. | New York—PARIS—London | 1 Fr. | Friday, Dec. 29, 1944

U.S. Gains on 35-Mi. Line

Churchill Nearly Hit By Sniper

ATHENS, Dec. 28.—Prime Minister Churchill and Foreign Minister Anthony Eden, after narrowly escaping assassination by a sniping machine-gunner, left for London today with a Greek peace formula in their pockets. It called for a regency to supplant King George II.

A burst from a hidden machine-gun had zipped past Churchill yesterday as the Prime Minister and his party stepped out of the British Embassy for an armored car tour of Athens. A Greek girl was killed just 30 yards away from him. The party, which included Eden, Field Marshal Sir Harold Alexander and Maj. Gen. Ronald M. Scobie, calmly proceeded with the tour.

Archbishop Likely Regent

A conference of the warring Greek political factions, brought together by Churchill, reached a unanimous decision favoring a regency and it was officially announced that Churchill and Eden would recommend its appointment to the Greek king in London, who heretofore has been opposed to one.

The regent probably would be Archbishop Damaskinos of the Greek Orthodox Church, an ardent anti-Fascist who is believed to be acceptable both to the left-wing EAM (resistance front) and the Rightists. Premier George Papandreou offered to resign.

The regency then would be faced with the task of reconciling the warring political factions. This Papandreou has failed to do, but conditions under which the regency would operate would be more favorable than those confronting the present government.

Big 3 to Review Situation

Before his departure, Churchill told a press conference that he, President Roosevelt and Marshal Stalin would review the Greek situation at an early meeting and that if the Greeks fail to solve their differences "an international trust might be necessary" to rule the country.

To the sound of sniper fire outside the embassy and the thud of British artillery shelling ELAS positions, Churchill declared determinedly that British armed intervention would not stop until the differences were settled "either by free negotiation or by the increasing use of military force." The British will not withdraw, he added, without "guarantees, in which we can believe, that a fair and decent government will be set up which will not pay off old scores on either side."

Where Americans Hack at Bulge

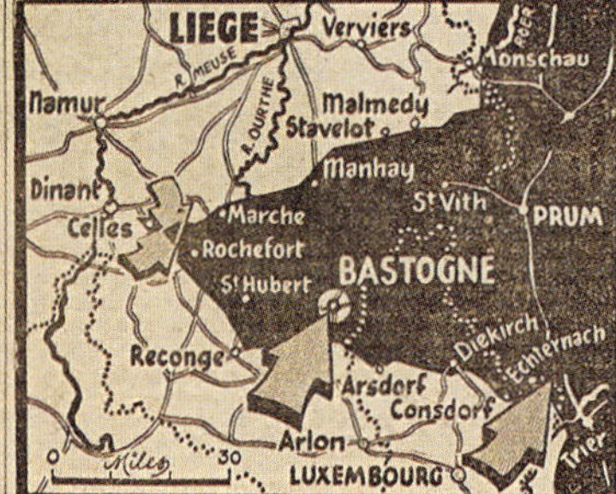

Stars and Stripes Map by Baird

American forces drive ten miles to relieve the Bastogne garrison, besieged for seven days, while German radio reports U.S. recapture of Echternach, on the Luxembourg-German border.

'Jerries Really Laid It On', Survivors Say of Nazi Push

By Charles Kiley
Stars and Stripes Staff Writer

The dynamite behind the German counter-offensive is gone, according to SHAEF. The advance is slowed down, and in some sectors Americans are moving up again with the balance of strength they lacked when their lines were forced to bend and yield under superior enemy power.

But Jim Williams and Abe Rich, a couple of doughfeet from an outfit that caught one of the first blows of the attack near the Luxembourg-Belgian border on the morning of Dec. 17, are around to testify that the Jerries really laid it on.

Williams, a communications platoon chief and staff sergeant from Harrisburg, Pa., and Rich, rifle company Pfc from [illegible] Park, N.Y., came out of the line yesterday with one of the first reports of the counter-offensive by those who stood in its path.

They told of regimental and battalion commanders, colonels, ma-

(Continued on Page 8)

Merchants Urged Not to Cheat GIs

Representatives of the French exporting industries adopted a unanimous resolution yesterday urging French merchants to charge Allied soldiers and French customers the same prices. The action was taken at a meeting to study trans-Atlantic business relations after the war.

At the same time the Paris newspaper Combat, commenting on a tendency it saw among some Frenchmen to berate the Americans for not bringing enough food and fuel for the civilians, reminded its readers that the Americans were giving something more precious—their lives.

Saying that most GIs seen in Paris were on their way to bloody battles, the newspaper commented: "There you have their Christmas gift—instead of chocolate."

Berchtesgaden Vacated

MOSCOW, Dec. 28 (UP).—Adolf Hitler is believed here to have abandoned his Berchtesgaden estate because of the advance of the Soviet Armies toward Austria, bringing the fighting front within 200 miles of his mountain hideout.

Nazis Retake Barga In Italy Offensive

15TH ARMY GROUP HQ., Dec. 28 (Reuter).—German troops who attacked in force in the mountainous west coast sector of the Italian front northeast of Leghorn have recaptured the small town of Barga, two and a half miles east of Gallicano on the Serchio River, and are continuing to press back leading Allied elements.

Springing suddenly from their snowbound mountain defenses, the Germans launched an offensive on a seven-mile front down both sides of the Serchio River and around the key road junction town of Gallicano, some 40 miles northeast of Leghorn, Fifth Army supply port.

Only meager details were released on the German drive, but it was officially admitted that slight withdrawals had been forced and some ground relinquished around Barga. This part of the Apennines was last announced as entrusted to the U.S. 92nd Div.

32,000 Held as Pro-Nazis

Frenchmen interned or imprisoned on suspicion of pro-Nazi activities now total 32,000, Interior Minister Tixier reported yesterday. Of these, 5,000 cases have not yet been investigated.

3d Army Cracks Bastogne Siege; Nazi Flank Reels

Field Marshal von Rundstedt's south flank appeared to be wobbling last night as official reports showed American forces which had driven 10 miles in five days to relieve Bastogne advancing along a 35-mile front. The siege was raised by a U.S. Third Army armored force.

As a pea-soup fog descended on the frozen hills of Eastern Belgium and Luxembourg, the Germans admitted for the first time that their 11th-hour blitz is on the defensive between Bastogne and Echternach.

German radio said last night that American troops had recaptured Echternach on the Luxembourg-German border.

Latest official battle reports, still 36 hours behind front developments, showed:

1. **Americans held their mile-wide corridor to Bastogne against the first strong Nazi counter-attack.**
2. **German armor patrolling toward the Meuse was mauled by Allied forces.**
3. **Powerful Nazi attacks between Stavelot and Marche toward Antwerp supply lines were smeared.**
4. **U.S. forces recaptured Grandmenil and Manhay in the west tip of the enemy bulge, according to U.P.**

The German Transocean Newsagency Correspondent, Guenther Weber, reported last night that the Germans had gone over to "an elastic defense" on the south flank which forms the belly of the bulge.

It was the first indication from an enemy source that the Christmas blitz had hit a snag.

Channelized by Allied pressure on its north and south flanks, the bulge was being squeezed as its western tentacles groped to within three miles of the northern bulge of France north of Charleville.

Yanks Cross Sure River

Sizable enemy forces in the vicinity of Ciney and Celles were reported. The whole western perimeter of the bulge was [illegible], with both U.S. and German tanks milling around without making any strong attacks.

In central Luxembourg, Americans crossed the Sure River in three places.

Northwest of Echternach, enemy troops were withdrawing back into

(Continued on Page 8)

Soviets Enter Buda Streets

MOSCOW, Dec. 28 (AP).—Red Army units, under clouds of smoke from burning buildings, pushed into the streets of Buda on the western bank of the Danube River today but in Pest they found grim resistance from suicide forces.

(The Berlin communiqué [illegible] that even as the Soviets fought to reduce Budapest itself they hurled strong new forces into a mounting offensive beyond the by-passed city, driving westward toward Austria.)

In Buda several streets already were in Russian hands. There was

(Continued on Page 8)

New Capes for GI Snow-Fighters

T/4 Marvin C. Eans, of Owensboro, Ky., demonstrates the snow cape now being issued First Army troops on the Western Front. White rags camouflage the rifle.

Army Again Orders Seizure Of Montgomery Ward Stores

WASHINGTON, Dec. 28 (ANS).—The War Department, acting on a Presidential edict, today ordered seizure of Montgomery Ward properties in seven cities after the nation's largest mail order house had refused to comply with War Labor Board directives.

It was the second major crack-down this year against the company. Last spring Ward Chairman Sewell Avery was physically ejected from his Chicago office.

Army troops this morning were moving to take over Ward properties in Chicago; St. Paul, Minn.; Jamaica, N.Y.; Kansas City; San Rafael, Calif. and Baltimore.

Yesterday in Chicago counters were broken, fixtures were smashed and goods thrown into aisles when a crowd swept through the Dearborn Ave. store after strike-breakers had attempted to interfere with picketing outside the store.

Ward's Chicago headquarters said that a court order designed to sustain the government action was expected to be filed in Federal district courts in areas of the cities

(Continued on Page 8)

Friday, Dec. 29, 1944 — THE STARS AND STRIPES — Page 7

Hash Marks

Who said that? The map of Europe is like a woman's mind—always ready for a battle and subject to change without notice.

* * *

Our spy on the home front heard this remark in a PX. "It's nice we're still living in a free country and a man can do what the first sergeant wants him to."

* * *

And then there was the Lieutenant who phoned his wife and said, "Sorry, dear, I won't be home until late. I have a form here I have to look over."

* * *

"My girl's sure carrying the torch for me." Sighed a GI.—"She's a welder at Lockheed."

* * *

Afterthought. The most popu-

lar GI corsage is still four roses.

* * *

Catty remark. "To that girl, dating is just like a drug—she takes one dope after another."

* * *

And then there was the discharged GI who landed a soft job. He's in a pantie factory now, pulling down about two thousand a year.

* * *

Another unsigned verse left in our typewriter:

Little paycheck, by tonight
We'll be where the lights are bright.
In some gaily festive spot
I'll return but you will not.

* * *

PFC Lou Seguin reported in the Weather Column of his "Daily Dope Sheet" that England had a long dry spell—one morning.

* * *

Someone asked a WAC how her Boyfriend in the engineers made love. She replied, "You can define it a unskilled labor."

* * *

Signs of the Times. Mistletoe sales dropped to a new low in the Midwest this season. One puzzled mistletoe magnate explained. "I guess they're just no one around worth kissing any more. We think he overlooked the fact that servicemen don't need the stuff.

* * *

Remark heard on the home front. "Go ahead and telephone, and if a man answers, ask him why the hell he isn't in the army."

J. C. W.

Help Wanted —AND GIVEN

Write your question or problem to Help Wanted, The Stars and Stripes, Paris, France. APO 887.

APOs WANTED

SGT. Willard Johnson; Cpl. Arthur Jackson; Pvt. A. Jacobson, New Hope, Pa.; Pvt. Harry Kaplan, Atlantic City; Sgt. Jim Landers, Tex.; Harold Lacey, Newark Valley, N.Y.; George Daniel Lane; Pvt. John J. Moran; Howard O. Maloney, Wilmington, Del.; Pvt. Amos Martin, Ohio; Neal J. Martinson, Passaic, N.Y.

PVT. Albert Morgan, N.Y.C.; John V. Murphy, Brooklyn; James and Edward Murdock, Pomfret, Conn.; William M. Moody; James H. McCarty, Philadelphia; Pvt. Ralph Morse, Lancaster, N.H.; Bob McCarthy, East Dubuque, Ill.

CPL. William Olson, Neb.; Duke Perry, Windsor, N.C.; George Pearson, Fargo; S/Sgt. Charles Rooney, Columbus, O.; Robert Ryan, Chicago; Pfc Irving Rubin; Fred Schaeffer, Milwaukee; Robert Smoots, Detroit; Leo Spiegler, Chicago; Lt. Chas. S. Stevens; Lt. David Thom and Lt. George Thom, Beechhurst, N.Y.; Jack Tucker, Lebanon, Ore.; Bob Tippins, Rochelle, Ga.; Sgt. Robert Terry; Cpl. Robert S. Wood, Fowler, Mich.; Sgt. Roger R. Waggoner, Nebraska.

AEF-RADIO Program-AFN

Time — TODAY

0925—AEF Ranch House.
1901—Command Performance.
1930—Kate Smith.
2030—Moonlight Serenade.

TOMORROW

1430—Kollege of Musical Knowledge.
1515—Record (Cpl. Geo. Monaghan).
2030—Frank Morgan.
[illegible]—Jubilee

Terry And The Pirates

By Courtesy of News Syndicate — By Milton Caniff

Jane

By Courtesy of The London Daily Mirror — By Norman Pett

Dick Tracy

By Courtesy of Chicago Tribune Syndicate Inc. — By Chester Gould

Abbie an' Slats

By Courtesy of United Features — By Raeburn Van Buren

Male Call

By Milton Caniff

Blondie

By Courtesy of King Features Syndicate — By Chic Young

BATTLE OF THE BULGE: COUNTERBLOW

TUESDAY 19 DECEMBER 1944–SUNDAY 28 JANUARY 1945

On 19 December, three days after the German offensive began, Eisenhower summoned Bradley, Patton and Lieutenant General Jacob Devers, 6th Army Group Commander, to a conference at Verdun. Montgomery was invited but sent his Chief of Staff, Major General Sir Francis de Guingand, which all the Americans took as an insult.

When asked how quickly he could turn his army 90 degrees from facing east to attacking north, Patton said two days. This astonished Eisenhower, who thought Patton was boasting. In fact Patton and his staff had done their homework and, with his front taken over by formations from Devers' army group in the south, he had seven divisions on the road north within 48 hours. Patton was in his element, revelling in the fact that the enemy had "stuck his head in the meat-grinder", and that he, Patton, had a hold of the handle.

> "Sir this is Patton talking. The last fourteen days have been straight hell. Rain, snow, more rain, more snow – and I'm beginning to wonder what's going on in your headquarters. Whose side are you on anyway?"
>
> **PATTON'S PRAYER**

Because the German offensive had cut Bradley's communications with the US First and Ninth Armies in the northern half of the bulge, Eisenhower rightly decided that Montgomery was to be given temporary command of Hodges and Simpson, leaving the bitterly disappointed Bradley with the southern part, and commanding Patton's Third Army only. With Patton firmly in the driving seat, Bradley had nothing to do, and for the rest of his life blamed Montgomery for suggesting the command arrangements, which he had not, and Eisenhower for betraying him. It marked the start of an unhappy episode in Allied relationships.

While Patton bulled north in appalling weather conditions to relieve Bastogne, Montgomery gripped the situation on the other side of the salient, including deploying Horrocks' XXX Corps to hold the Meuse river crossings at Namur, Dinant and Givet. He was absolutely confident that by "boxing clever", using his head and not his emotions, the Germans would be defeated. His confidence seemed to the Americans like cockiness, he arrived in Hodges's HQ, said one, "like Christ coming to cleanse the temple".

BATTLE OF THE BULGE

BATTLE CASUALTIES IN TOTAL:

AMERICAN LOSSES:
75,522 out of which 8,477 killed, 46,170 wounded, 20,905 captured or missing in action (MIA)

BRITISH LOSSES:
1,408 out of which 200 killed, 239 wounded, 969 captured or MIA

GERMAN LOSSES:
86,675 out of which 19,749 killed, 34,439 wounded, 32,487 captured or MIA

BELGIAN AND LUXEMBOURGEOIS CIVILIAN LOSSES:
3,800 (approximately)

LEFT British 51st Highland Infantry Division badge.

LEFT US 84th Infantry Division badge.

TOP Americans meet up with the British in La Roche on 11 January. Left to right: Harlan Mathis (US), Harris McAlister (UK), Bill Towler (UK), Ray Spangler (US), John Donald (UK) and Rex Beal (US). The Americans were attached to the 84th Infantry Division; the British were from 5th Black Watch, 51st Highland Division.

ABOVE A Mk IV destroyed by 37th Glider Infantry, 101st Airborne Division, during attack by Kampfgruppe Maucke of 15th Panzer Grenadier Division on the western side of the Bastogne perimeter on Christmas morning.

ABOVE Troopers of the US 3rd Armored Division in the vicinity of Hoton on the northern shoulder of the Bulge, awaiting orders to advance down the Liege-Bastogne Road.

On Boxing Day, Patton relieved Bastogne. To the north-west, at the very point of the German salient, the leading elements of 2nd Panzer Division waited for fuel on high ground overlooking the Meuse at Dinant, the rest of the division stacked up behind them. Major General Ernest Harmon's entire 2nd Armoured Division of Collins's VII Corps struck like the crack of doom, utterly crushing 2nd Panzer Division and troops that tried to come to their assistance.

Over Christmas week the weather that had been foul, cleared, and once more the skies were filled with Allied aircraft pounding the Germans wherever they found them. The fighting was not over, and the bulge was not squeezed out until 28 January. It had cost the Germans dear, more than 100,000 men and some 800 tanks. It was the greatest pitched battle fought by the Americans in their history, and to the American soldier belongs the credit for the crushing defeat inflicted on the Germans.

BELOW The end of the dream, German bodies discovered in late January near the Belgian-Luxembourg border.

26 DECEMBER 1944–7 FEBRUARY 1945

BATTLE OF THE BULGE

KEY

- Front line 26 December 1944
- Front line 9 January 1945
- Front line 24 January 1945
- Front line 7 February 1945

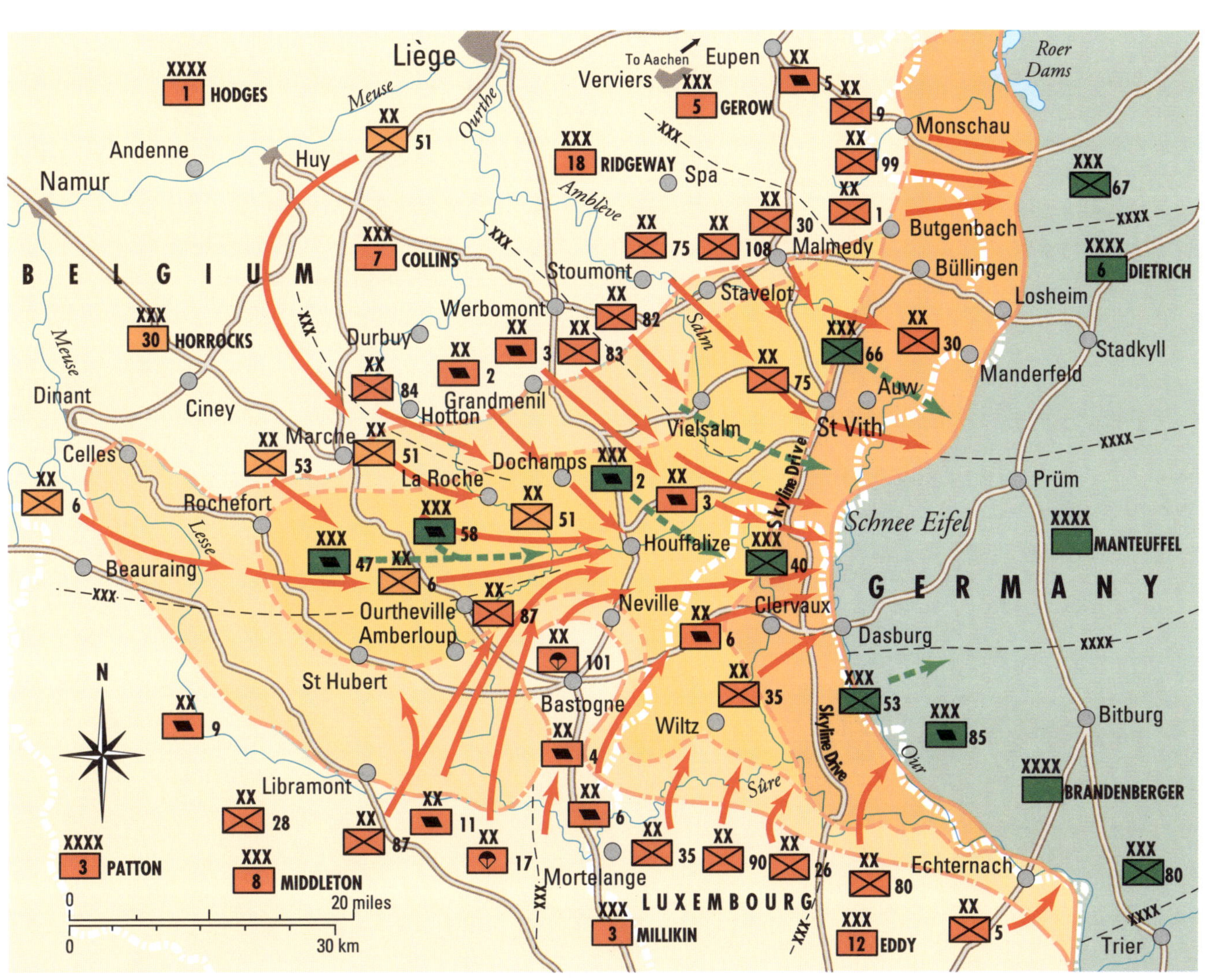

THE YALTA CONFERENCE

SUNDAY 4 FEBRUARY–SUNDAY 11 FEBRUARY 1945

President Roosevelt, Winston Churchill and Stalin met at Yalta in the Crimea from 4–11 February 1945, ostensibly to discuss future strategy and the division of post-war Germany. Much of the discussion and agreement was on a bilateral basis between Roosevelt and Stalin, reflecting the diminishing role of Britain in the war compared with the United States and the Soviet Union.

In hindsight, it is clear that the three leaders had widely differing objectives. Stalin aimed to expand Russia's empire to ensure her security. Roosevelt wanted to win Russia's friendship by charming Stalin, and set up a United Nations organization that would reduce the risk of international conflict for evermore. Meanwhile, Churchill hoped to defeat Germany and prevent the Soviet Union from becoming too powerful.

There was agreement by all three leaders on an Allied Control Commission for Germany and that France should be one of the occupying powers. Although on the latter point Stalin insisted that the French sector should come from the UK and US Zones, not the Soviet one.

There was discussion on the future of Poland that ended in a betrayal of this gallant nation that had fought from the outbreak of war in 1939, and maintained the fourth largest army among those nations opposed to Germany. Poland's eastern provinces were transferred to Russia, and Soviet domination of Poland was tacitly accepted. It could be argued that this Roosevelt-Stalin deal reflected reality, since Russia already occupied all of Poland. But the Poles and Churchill saw it as treachery.

LEFT The coast of the Crimea where the conference took place. Churchill called it the "Riviera of Hades".

BERLIN

Well before Yalta it had been agreed that the Russians would occupy eight boroughs in the north-east part of Berlin, the British six in the north-west and the Americans six in the south-west. At Yalta Stalin said that the French share must come from the British and/or American sectors. By the Potsdam conference in July 1945, the French still had no sector. The Russians refused to give up anything. The impasse was solved by the British handing the French two of their boroughs.

Stalin made clear that he wanted Germany completely dismembered, and intended to strip Geman industry as a recompense for the damage done by the Germans in the Soviet Union.

The most important deal concluded at Yalta, directly between Roosevelt and Stalin was over the future of the war in the Pacific. In order to get Russia into the war gainst Japan (the Soviet Union was not at war with Japan), Roosevelt not only handed Poland's future to Russia (although he did not see it that way at the time), but also agreed to Russia occupying the biggest slice of Germany, as well as telling Stalin he could have Manchuria. Bear in mind, that at the stage Roosevelt made these concessions, the United States had not successfully tested an atomic bomb, and the prospect of years of bloody fighting loomed ahead. At that time the anticipated date for the end of the war against Japan was late 1946 or even 1947. Roosevelt wanted the Russians to take part in the invasion of Japan, and if the price for saving American lives in the Pacific was letting down the Poles, the Chinese and Churchill, so be it.

> "The Polish Question is a question of life or death for the Soviet State."
>
> **STALIN**

Within days of the end of the Yalta conference, Stalin had installed a puppet prime minister in Rumania. Following the end of the war in Europe, regardless of what had been agreed at Yalta, Stalin dealt with those territories liberated by the Red Army entirely to his own satisfaction. There was no progress to the reorganization of the Polish Provisional Government "on a more democratic basis" as agreed at Yalta. He ultimately gained every one of his objectives, save one, control of the Black Sea Straits.

Yalta, and especially the Anglo/American concessions to Stalin, which he saw as weakness, shaped the world until the Berlin Wall came down in 1989, and to some extent still does.

LEFT Final dinner of the Yalta conference, in the centre, left to right: Stalin, Roosevelt and Churchill. With extreme left Edward R. Stettinius, US Secretary of State, and extreme right Molotov, Russian Foreign Minister.

ABOVE The "Big Three" with their advisors at the Yalta conference.

CHURCHILL *was one of the most successful war leaders in British history. He had seen war first hand, and was a talented and very experienced politician. His loathing of Nazism, and deep attachment to democracy were evident in his marvellous oratory. He harried his senior commanders and officials, especially if he thought they were being inefficient or timid. Aged 70 by 1944, he survived many long, exhausting and dangerous journeys during the war. His watchword was "Action this day."*

ROOSEVELT *had been President of the United States for nearly 12 years at the time of Yalta, having just begun an unprecedented and never to be repeated fourth term of office. He has been criticised for the concessions he made to Stalin at Yalta, but with Churchill, he was one of the architects of victory in the Second World War. As such, his contribution to the survival of world democracy is beyond doubt. He died on 12 April 1945, never seeing the peace.*

STALIN *was the only Allied leader who held office throughout the war. As the Yalta Conference broke up, with the Soviet armies on the Oder and Danube, and Western Allies on the Rhine, the race for Berlin was on as far as Stalin was concerned and he cracked the whip over his generals. His "Uncle Joe" image in America and Britain was belied by his cruelty to his own people, including liquidating thousands of his own soldiers and "suspect" ethnic groups.*

ALLIED OCCUPATION ZONES (AS AGREED AT YALTA)

KEY

- Controlled by Four Power Commission
- British
- American
- French
- Russian
- Russian Administration
- Polish Administration

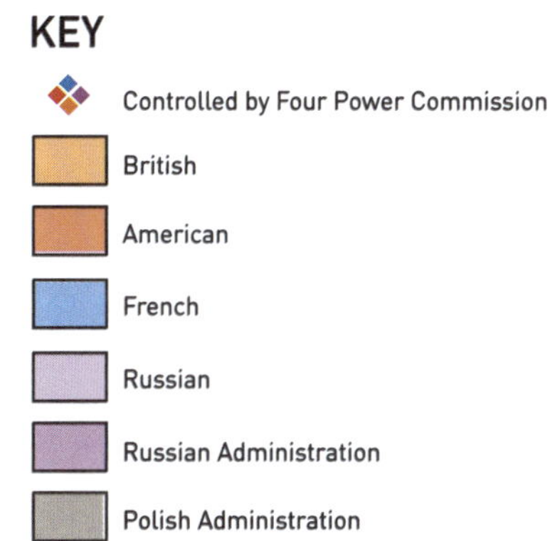

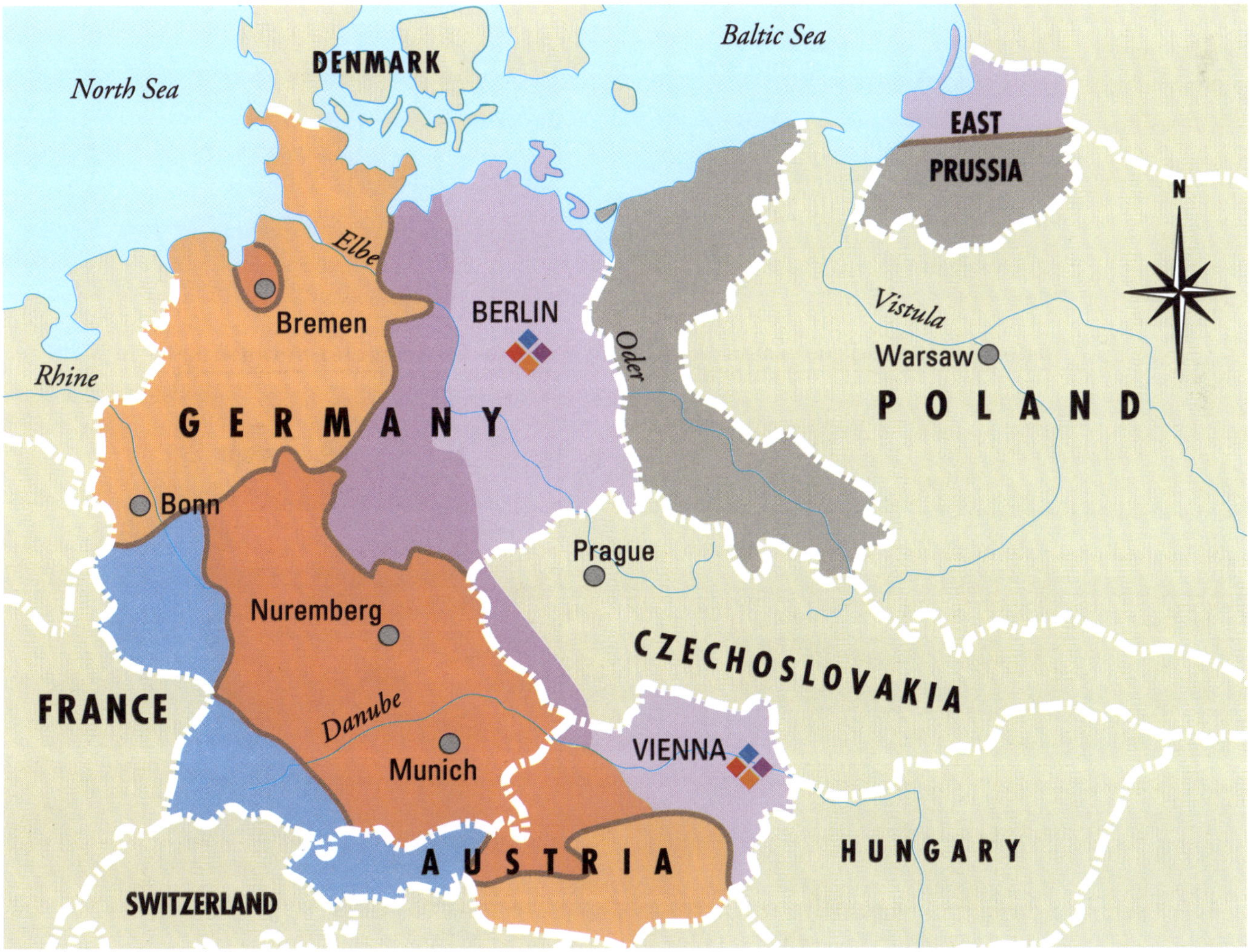

BREAKING THE SIEGFRIED LINE

THURSDAY 8 FEBRUARY–MONDAY 5 MARCH 1945

By the end of January 1945, the scene was set for the Battle of the Rhineland: securing the ground between the Meuse (called the Maas in the north) and the Rhine as a prelude to crossing the Rhine itself. The Siegfried Line, consisting of concrete pillboxes, anti-tank ditches and "dragon's teeth" obstacles, augmented by minefields, defended the Rhineland. Flooding and forest added to the daunting problems facing the attacker. But thanks to the huge losses of German troops in the Battle of the Bulge, the Allies encountered

LOWER RHINELAND CASUALTIES

ALLIES:

US: 7,300
British/Canadian: 15,600

AXIS:

52,000 POWs. (numbers of dead and wounded unknown)

BELOW Soldiers moving cautiously through the Reichswald Forest where Canadian and British troops had a tough fight.

ABOVE British troops winkling out the last pockets of enemy resistance in Cleve supported by tanks.

FAR LEFT 15th Scottish Infantry Division badge.

LEFT British 43rd Wessex Infantry Division badge.

"A Company had twenty-four killed; and many wounded. B Company were ordered to carry out the second phase. Very few prisoners were taken."

LIEUTENANT WALTER CAINES 4TH DORSETS, 15 FEBRUARY, REICHSWALD

fewer defenders than they otherwise would have done, had the Germans not committed such a strategic blunder. This was fortunate since the fighting that ensued was tough enough without having to take on the Germans in the full flush of their power.

In the north, Montgomery with Canadian First Army and Lieutenant General William Simpson's US Ninth Army was to attack first. On 8 February, as planned by Montgomery, Canadian First Army attacked south from the Nijmegen salient, between the Maas and the Rhine, with British XXX Corps, under Canadian command, in the lead (Operation Veritable). This led behind the Siegfried line once the northern end had been breached. As XXX Corps cleared some elbow room, Canadian II Corps came up alongside and both corps headed for Geldern and Wesel.

ABOVE American soldiers of the First and Ninth US Armies on the Inde River training with flat-bottomed assault boats for the attack across the Roer River.

TOP Some of the 114 Bofors 40mm light anti-aircraft guns from two anti-aircraft brigades, which took part in the battle for Cleve in the ground-support role.

7 FEBRUARY–25 MARCH 1945

THE SIEGFRIED LINE

KEY

Front line 8 February
Front line 25 March
Siegfried Line

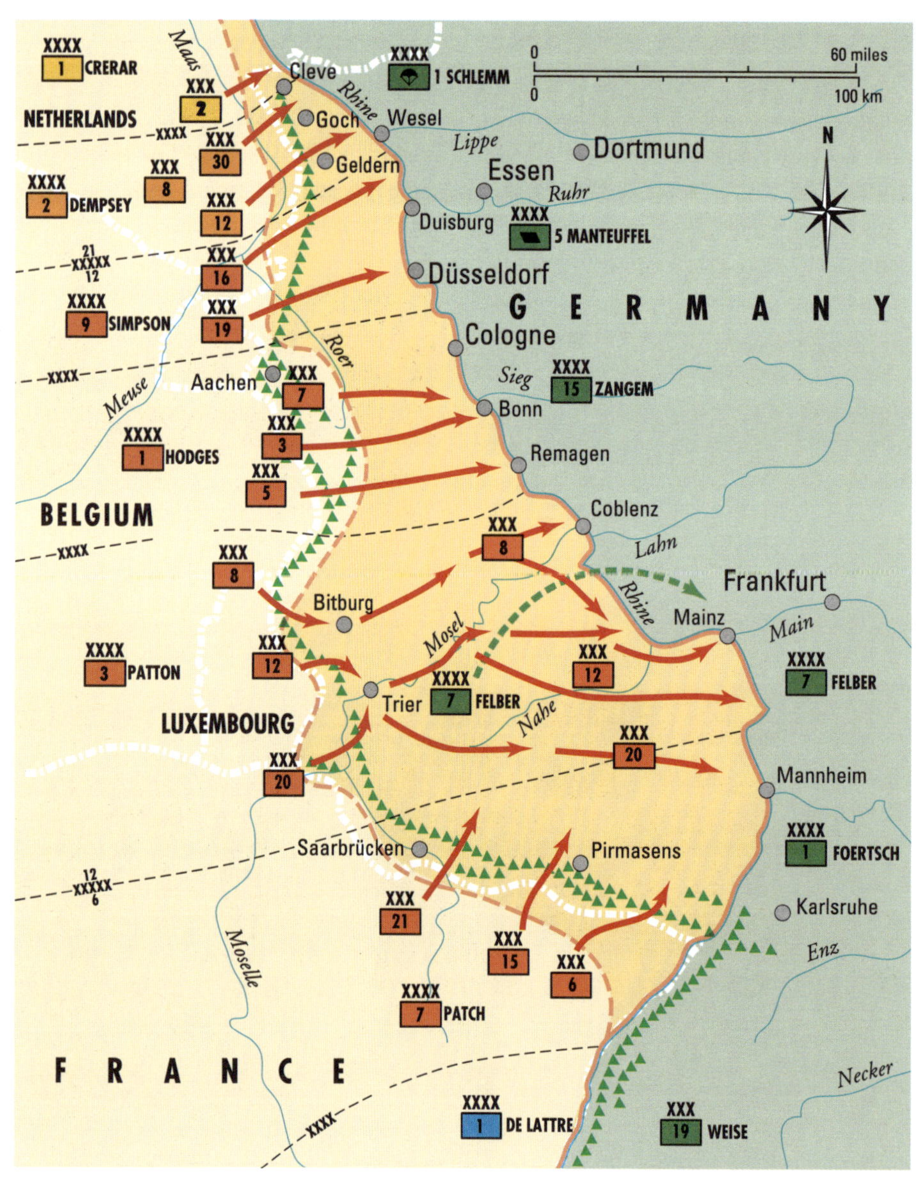

LIEUTENANT GENERAL WILLIAM H. SIMPSON

was a classmate of Patton at West Point. Graduating second from bottom, he commanded an infantry battalion with distinction in the First World War and rose to command the US Ninth Army in Europe, where he became one of the US Army's most brilliant generals. He was especially known for being able to work well with Montgomery. Simpson joked to Patton that though older than Bradley and Ike, they were "carrying the ball for those two sons of bitches".

ABOVE German prisoners marched through the "dragon's teeth" of the Siegfried Line after being captured by the US 36th Infantry Division of the Seventh Army.

LEFT US Ninth Army badge.

First, the Canadians and British had to clear the Reichswald forest, a formidable obstacle on the western end of the Siegfried Line. The ground had thawed and soon became a quagmire, but the Canadians and 30 Corps made good progress initially. Fighting through the rubble-strewn streets of Cleve by 15th (Scottish) and 43rd (Wessex) Divisons slowed up momentum, and the Reichswald was not cleared until 13 February. The Germans were able to concentrate on trying to contain the Canadian offensive because the Ninth Army, the other pincer of Monty's offensive, was still held behind the flooded Roer River. Monty's plan was for Simpson to attack (Operation Grenade) 48 hours after the start of Veritable, but thanks to the flooding, the operation was postponed.

By 23 February, the floods in the Roer valley had subsided, and Simpson headed north over drying ground in fine weather. On 3 March, British armour of the 4/7th Dragoon Guards in Canadian First Army linked up with tanks of the Ninth Army at Geldern, before both armies made for the Rhine, reaching it on 11 March.

In the south, Bradley's US 12th Army Group (First and Third Armies) was also heading through the Siegfried Line for the Rhine. By 5 March, Hodges's First Army's V Corps had taken the western part of Cologne, to find all the bridges demolished. The remainder of First Army headed south-east for Bonn and Remagen to take the Germans in the Eifel in the rear. Patton's Third Army crashed straight through the wooded hills of the Eifel, taking only three days to cover the 56 miles to Coblenz, where the Rhine and Moselle meet.

The British, Canadians and Americans now breasted up to the mighty Rhine, where it seemed that every bridge had been destroyed.

ABOVE Soldiers of the US 84th Division, Ninth US Army enter Erkelenz after crossing the Roer on 23 February.

NOT TO BE USED FOR SHOOTING
SECRET
OPERATION VERITABLE
COMBINED FIRE PLAN OVERPRINT SHEET I
BARRAGE SHOWN IN PURPLE
15(S) DIV TARGETS SHOWN IN RED
51(H) DIV TARGETS SHOWN IN BLACK
53(W) DIV TARGETS SHOWN IN BLUE
SMOKE SCREENS SHOWN IN GREEN
COMPOSITE MAP
PARTS OF GSGS 4427 SHEETS 6SW 12NW 12SW
OF GSGS 4414 SHEETS 4102 4202
Kranenburg
Groesbeek
Nutterden
Zyfflich
Wyler
Mehr
LEFT
EDWARD
RIGHT
PAUSE
BARGE
ARK
CRUISER
CORVETTE
DESTROYER
MONITOR
SCHOONER
SKIFF
LINER ONE
LINER TWO
PUNT
FRIGATE
R E I C H

OPPOSITE Corps artillery barrage map for Operation "Veritable".

BELOW The transparent overlay for the map enabled the plan to be amended and extra targets to be plotted as required.

INDEX NO. 3.

OPERATION "VERITABLE"

R.A. 30 CORPS FIRE PLAN : BARRAGE

Ref. Maps. Holland 1:25.000 Sheets 12NW (East) 4102. 4202.

Issued in conjunction with Task Tables 33a, 33b, 33c

SECRET

5 Feb. 45.

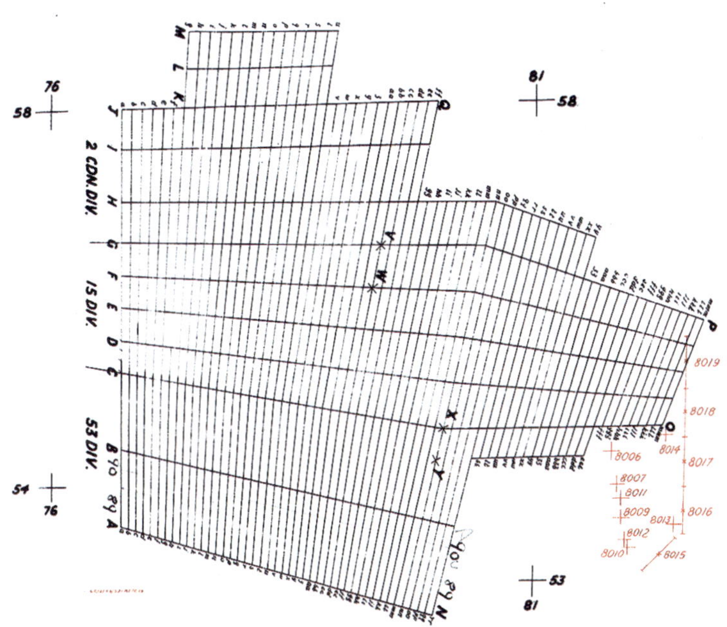

Co-ordinates.

A.	476720	553610	22m.
J.	476720	558000	44m.
N.	479920	552680	23m.
O.	482260	554610	33m.
P.	482670	555680	12m.
Q.	479960	557980	11m.

15 Div Concs. and D.F. Tasks are shown in red
(Separate Task Tables for these are being issued)

THE BRIDGE AT REMAGEN

WEDNESDAY 7 MARCH–SATURDAY 17 MARCH 1945

At 1.00 p.m., on 7 March 1945, Second Lieutenant Emmet Burrows commanding the leading elements of a task force from Combat Command B (CCB), 9th Armored Division, III Corps, reached high bluffs overlooking Remagen, below him the Ludendorff railway bridge over the Rhine stood intact. He summoned his company commander, Lieutenant Karl Timmerman, who reported that the bridge was intact to the task force commander, Lieutenant Colonel Leonard Engeman. Down at the bridge, although the Germans knew that the Americans were on the bluffs above, there was uncertainty and disagreement about exactly when the bridge was to be blown.

LIEUTENANT KARL TIMMERMAN, *the first American officer across the Rhine, already had a connection with Remagen. His father was in the US occupation force in Germany in 1919, where he married a local girl from Remagen, and took her back to his native Nebraska where Timmerman was born.*

LEFT The Ludendorff railway bridge over the River Rhine at Remagen seen from the west bank, the direction from which Lieutenant Timmerman and his company approached. The railway went into a tunnel through on the opposite bank.

ABOVE US 9th Armored Division badge.

"Hot dog, Courtney. This will bust him wide open. Shove everything you can across it."

GENERAL BRADLEY TO GENERAL COURTNEY HODGES ON HEARING OF THE TAKING OF THE REMAGEN BRIDGE.

Engeman was ordered by Brigadier General William Hoge, the CCB commander, to get his task force to the bridge as soon as possible. Having fought through the town, Timmerman's infantrymen, with a platoon of tanks, neared the bridge at about 4.00 p.m. At this point, a German engineer, Captain Karl Friesenhahn on his own initiative blew a charge on the bridge approaches, in a vain attempt to stop tanks getting closer. Pandemonium reigned on the German side while Major Hans Scheller, Captain Willi Bratge and Friesenhahn argued over whom had authority to blow the bridge. Both Bratge and Freisenhahn insisted on getting the order in writing.

Finally, Freisenhahn turned the key, nothing happened. Clearly the circuit was broken. A team rushed out to ignite the charge by hand. At last it detonated, but although the structure lifted in the huge explosion, when the dust and smoke cleared the bridge was still there.

Timmerman's men skirmished forward, bobbing and weaving, dashing from the cover of one girder to the next, the riflemen covered by tanks on the western bank, crossed the bridge. Close behind came engineers who cut every wire in sight. The first American across was Sergeant Drabik; a moment later came Timmerman.

In the railway tunnel on the German side, Major Scheller having tried in vain to contact his headquarters to report that the bridge was intact, mounted a bicycle and peddled off to report in person. Captain Bratge and Captain Friesenhahn surrendered to the Americans.

Combat engineers worked hard to fit heavy planking and beams to enable their tanks to cross. Within 24 hours most of a division was across with supporting armour. Just over a day later engineers had constructed a pontoon bridge and a floating treadway bridge.

ABOVE Soon after the capture of the Remagen Bridge, US engineers laying planking and hardcore across the railway tracks to enable tracked and wheeled vehicles to cross.

CROSS THE RHINE WITH DRY FEET
COURTESY OF 9TH ARMD DIV.
MP

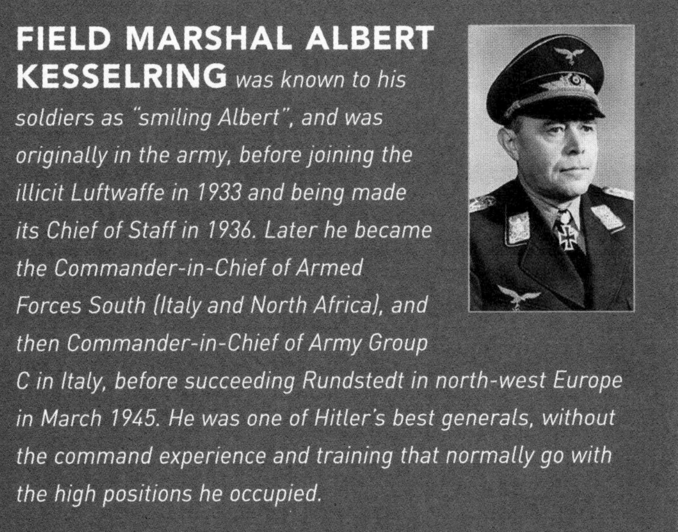

FIELD MARSHAL ALBERT KESSELRING *was known to his soldiers as "smiling Albert", and was originally in the army, before joining the illicit Luftwaffe in 1933 and being made its Chief of Staff in 1936. Later he became the Commander-in-Chief of Armed Forces South (Italy and North Africa), and then Commander-in-Chief of Army Group C in Italy, before succeeding Rundstedt in north-west Europe in March 1945. He was one of Hitler's best generals, without the command experience and training that normally go with the high positions he occupied.*

The Germans made several efforts to destroy the bridge, including using swimmers with charges, and the first and only tactical use of V-2 rockets, but none did any damage. On 17 March, Lieutenant General Hodges telephoned Major General John Millikin, the commander of III Corps, to tell him the bad news that he was being sacked because in his view he was not exploiting the capture of the bridge fast enough. Millikin had some bad news for his army commander, the bridge, possibly weakened by bombing, shelling, and heavy traffic, suddenly collapsed, killing 28 US engineers and wounding 93. The loss of the bridge had no effect on operations in the Remagen bridgehead. A greater mystery is why the main charge failed to detonate; some believe a tank shell cut the cord.

On Hitler's orders four German officers, including Major Scheller, were tried by court martial and executed for allowing the bridge to fall intact in to American hands. Hitler also removed Field Marshal von Rundstedt from command of all German troops in the West, replacing him with Field Marshal Albert Kesselring from Italy.

The seizure of the Remagen Bridge was a brilliant example of American initiative and speed of reaction. By 13 March three US infantry divisions (9th, 78th and 99th) were in the bridgehead. But Eisenhower was not able to exploit this coup fully, because, being committed to a main effort north of the Ruhr he had few reserves to spare for Remagen.

OPPOSITE TOP LEFT An American military policeman by one of the stone towers of the Ludendorff Bridge.

OPPOSITE TOP RIGHT American infantry and armor advances over the hardcore laid between the railway tracks on the Remagen Bridge, passing German prisoners being herded back over the Rhine.

OPPOSITE Quadruple barrelled tracked anti-aircraft guns protect the Remagen Bridge from German air attacks.

ABOVE On 17 March, as 200 US engineers worked on the bridge, there were two sharp reports, the decking vibrated and swayed, and with a roar of tearing steel the bridge plunged into the Rhine.

OPERATIONS PLUNDER AND VARSITY

FRIDAY 23–WEDNESDAY 28 MARCH 1945

On the night 23–24 March, two Armies under Field Marshal Montgomery crossed the Rhine between Rheinberg and Rees, the US Ninth on the right British Second on the left. 59,000 engineers supported the two armies, and 1,900 guns. In the three days preceding the attack the RAF flew over 5,000 sorties and the USAAF over 11,000. Specialised armour of Hobart's 79th Armoured Division played a key part in the river crossing, as did a flotilla of landing craft transported by road across Belgium and Holland.

At 9.00 p.m. the assault waves of four battalions of the 51st Highland Division entered the water in their Buffaloes, and seven minutes later they were on the far bank. Soon the Division was approaching the outskirts of Rees. On Second Army's right, the 1st Commando Brigade crossed at 10.00 p.m. west of Wesel. The Brigade waited for fifteen minutes while two hundred Lancasters dropped 1,000 tons of bombs a mere 1,500 yards ahead of the leading commandos, before entering the town at 3.00 a.m. After fierce fighting, the commandos eliminated the German defenders. By this time the leading battalions of the 15th Division were across at Xanten. In the Ninth Army sector, the US 30th and 79th Divisions crossed successfully and with light casualties.

Now it was the turn of British 6th and US 17th Airborne Divisions forming Major General Ridgway's 18th US Airborne Corps under command of Second Army. The Airborne Corps was tasked with

OPERATIONS PLUNDER & VARSITY

ALLIES

RIVER CROSSING ASSAULT FORMATIONS:

H-hour: Division H-Hours between 21.00 hours 23 March and 03.00 hours 24 March

- British 15th and 51st Divisions
- British 1st Commando Brigade
- US 30th and 79th Divisions

AIRBORNE ASSAULT:

P-hour: 10.00 hours 24 March

XVIII US Airborne Corps:

- British 6th Airborne Division
- US 17th Airborne Division

Aircraft to lift in Airborne Divisions and in support:

- 1,696 transport aircraft
- 1,348 gliders and tugs
- 889 escorting fighters
- 240 supply dropping aircraft
- 2,153 fighters maintaining umbrella

AXIS

EAST BANK AND IMMEDIATE VICINITY:

Five infantry divisions, two panzer divisions, one parachute division and elements, one infantry division.

AVAILABLE FOR COUNTER-ATTACK:

LXVII Panzer Corps of two panzer divisions, one panzer grenadier division and one infantry division disrupting the defence of the Rhine in the Wesel sector by seizing key terrain, and rapidly expanding the bridgehead formed by ground forces crossing the river, and then to assist the further offensive operations by the Second Army.

By mounting the airborne operation after the assault across the Rhine, the drop would be in daylight and most of the artillery would be on call to support the airborne soldiers. The DZs and LZs were chosen to be within artillery range of the 1,900 allied guns on the west bank. A link up of airborne and ground troops was planned for the first day. Learning another lesson from Arnhem, the DZs and LZs were all close to the objectives.

ABOVE With shovel and Sten gun, a lance-corporal of the 15th Scottish Division leads his section out of an assault boat on to the east bank of the Rhine.

RIGHT Infantry silhouetted against tracer and artificial moonlight – "Monty's moonlight" – as the Rhine crossing begins.

LIEUTENANT GENERAL MATTHEW RIDGWAY

was the first commander of the 82nd Airborne Division, which he led in Sicily, Italy, and Normandy, where he was always in the thick of the fighting. In August 1944 he was appointed to command XVIII Airborne Corps, subsequently directing operations in the Ardennes, the Rhine crossing, the Ruhr pocket, the Elbe crossing and the dash to the Baltic. According to him, losing his pistol after the drop in Normandy was his most embarrassing moment of the war.

In fine weather on the morning of 24 March, nearly 1,500 Dakotas and almost the same number of towing gliders brought in the British 6th and US 17th Divisions. Brigadier Hill's 3rd Parachute Brigade was on the DZ close to their objective in nine minutes. Within forty minutes the complete British 6th Airborne Division had landed. The landing by US 17th Airborne Division was similarly successful. By the end of the day 6th Airborne had seized Hamminkeln and the bridges over the River Issel, and 17th Airborne had taken Diersfordt and the wooded ground to the east, as well as further crossings over the Issel.

The 1st Commando Brigade linked up with 17th Airborne in Wesel, and 15th Division met 6th Airborne south-east of Mehr. The operation was a classic use of airborne troops, but costly. Over 50 gliders and 44 Dakotas were destroyed, and 332 damaged.

TOP Muzzle-flash from a British 5.5 medium gun lights up the sky as 1,900 guns fire in support of the assault across the Rhine.

ABOVE An American towed 105 mm gun follows other vehicles including a bulldozer across a pontoon bridge over the Rhine.

23–24 MARCH 1945

OPERATIONS PLUNDER AND VARSITY

KEY

- Front line 07.00 hours
- Front line 17.00 hours
- Allied artillery
- DZ Parachute drop zone
- LZ Glider landing zone

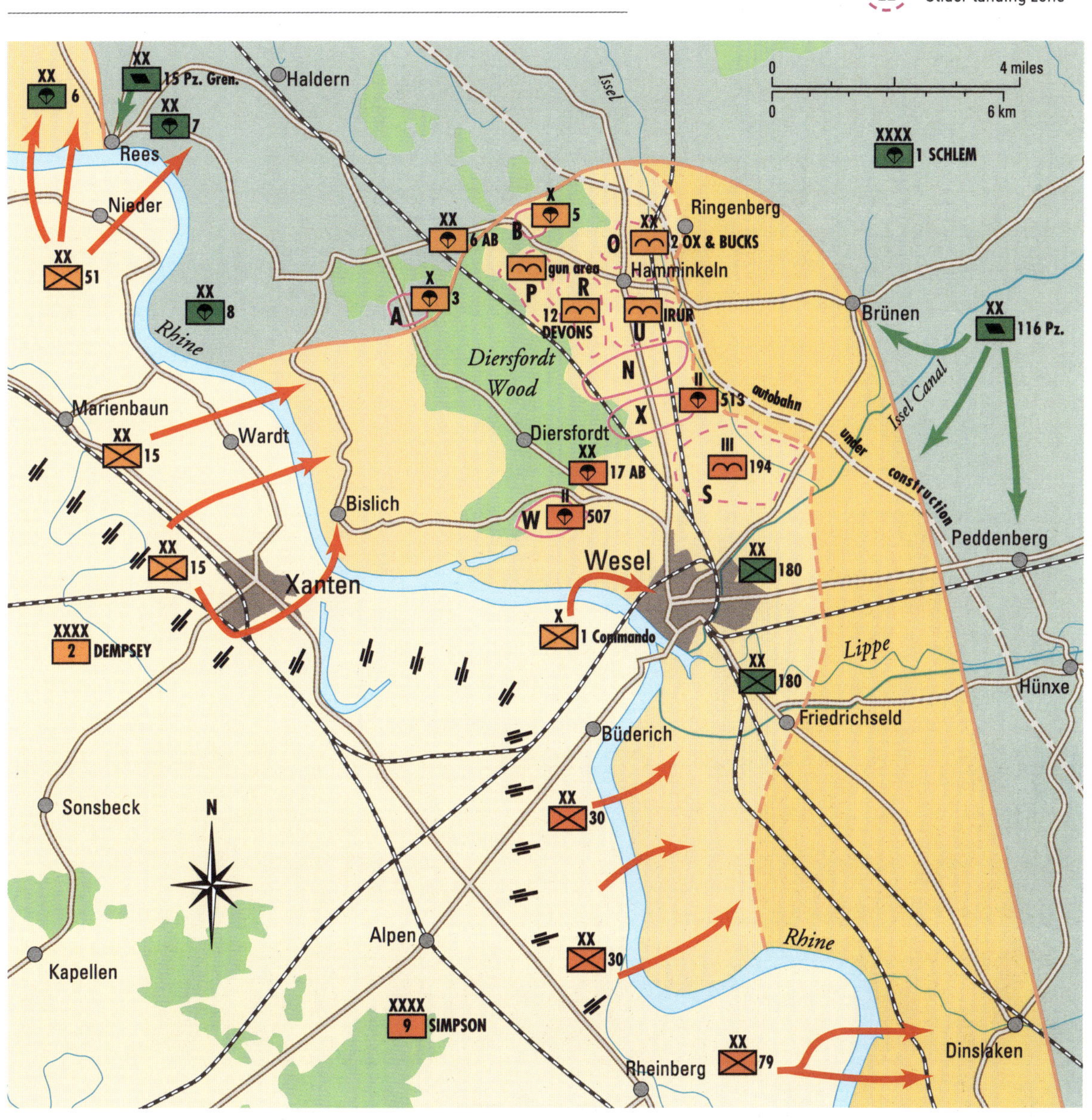

"And having crossed the Rhine, we will crack about on the plains of Northern Germany, chasing the enemy from pillar to post."

MONTGOMERY'S MESSAGE TO 21ST ARMY GROUP

ABOVE Number 6 Commando, British 1st Commando Brigade in Wesel among the rubble caused by bombs dropped from 2,000 Lancasters a few hours earlier. Some soldiers have Thompson sub-machine guns.

ABOVE RIGHT Paratroopers of Ridgway's XVIII Airborne Corps dropping on to DZs on the east bank of the Rhine on the morning after the river crossing by infantry.

TOP US 17th Airborne Division badge.

LEFT Breakout from the Rhine bridgehead, paratroopers of the 513th Parachute Infantry, US 17th Airborne Division on a Churchill tank of the British 6th Guards Tank Brigade heading towards Munster.

RIGHT "For Freedom and Life". A recruitment poster for the Volkssturm. A final attempt to make good the Wehrmacht's huge losses with "old men and boys".

BELOW Announcement to British forces written by Winston Churchill on the day of the airborne assault across the Rhine while he was on a visit to Montgomery's headquarters accompanied by the Chief of the Imperial General Staff, Field Marshal Sir Alan Brooke. He crossed the Rhine with Montgomery and Brooke in an American amphibious vehicle the same day.

~~HEADQUARTERS~~:

21 ARMY GROUP.

B.L.A.

24th March, 1945.

" I rejoice to be with the Chief of the Imperial General Staff at Field Marshal Montgomery's Headquarters of 21 Army Group ~~at~~ during this memorable battle of forcing the Rhine. British Soldiers - it will long be told how, with our Canadian brothers and valiant United States Allies, this superb task was accomplished. Once the river line is pierced and the crust of German resistance is broken decisive victory in Europe will be near. May God prosper our arms in this noble adventure after our long struggle for King and Country, for dear life, and for the freedom of mankind. "

Winston S. Churchill

Prime Minister & Minister of Defence

BELOW A 20-Mark note printed in the USA by the American Bank Note Company and used as currency by the Allied forces in occupied Germany.

ENCIRCLEMENT OF THE RUHR

MONDAY 26 MARCH–WEDNESDAY 18 APRIL 1945

As soon as Montgomery's 21st Army Group was across the Rhine, US Ninth Army reverted to Bradley's command for his drive through into Central Germany. The Third and Seventh US Armies had crossed the Rhine two days before Montgomery, and following the earlier Remagen crossing, there were now 90 Allied Divisions, nearly 4.5 million men, poised to administer the final blows to the western part of Hitler's Reich.

Field Marshal Model, commanding *Army Group B*, was convinced that Hodges's US First Army would break out of the Remagen bridgehead in a northerly direction and make straight for the Ruhr, the industrial heart of Germany. So he concentrated Fifth and Fifteenth Panzer Armies on the northern sector of the bridgehead. He was wrong, making Hodges' task easy when he broke out on 26 March heading east and south-east to link up with Patton's Third Army. With Patton protecting his right flank, Hodges curved around, heading north for Paderborn, a link-up with Simpson's Ninth Army, and complete encirclement of the Ruhr.

Hodges's armour advanced 45 miles in two days, one division taking over 12,000 prisoners in a day. Hodges's advance cut off General von Zangen's Fifteenth Army headquarters from Model and the remainder of Army Group B in the Ruhr. Model soon discerned that Hodges was heading for Paderborn thus trapping Army Group B. Any hope of Fifteenth Army coming to Army Group B's rescue evaporated

ENCIRCLEMENT OF THE RHUR

AXIS LOSSES

Seven corps and 19 divisions trapped in the Ruhr pocket.

323,000 Germans surrendered, more than the total taken at Stalingrad by the Russians

At least 24 generals captured

LEFT Wreathed in dust and smoke from artillery and tank fire, infantry and armour of Patton's US Third Army waiting to advance into Frankfurt. The soldier standing behind the tree has a bazooka slung over his shoulder.

FIELD MARSHAL WALTHER MODEL *never faltered in his loyalty to Hitler. After the July 1944 attempt on Hitler had failed, Model sent him a message vowing eternal allegiance. A ruthless, energetic man, he was not afraid to stand up to Hitler. Promoted to field marshal after stabilizing Army Group North's front in Russia in March 1944, the third time he had saved the situation on the Eastern Front, he acquired the nickname "the Führer's Fireman". He replaced Field Marshal Guenther Hans von Kluge as commander of Army Group B.*

ABOVE Infantry of the US Seventh Army search for snipers in Ludwigshafen.

when American armour rolled past von Zangen's headquarters and the luckless general fled to the forest with the remnants of his army. Hitler forbade withdrawal on pain of death, Model would have to stand and die in the Ruhr.

An SS training and reinforcement regiment from the training camp at Paderborn with sixty Panther and Tiger tanks bitterly contested

RIGHT The Hellcat was fast (50 mph), and with a high-velocity 76mm gun was well suited to the shoot 'n scoot tactics of the Tank Destroyer Command. Although popular, crews in the open-topped turret were vulnerable to overhead fire.

BELOW Troops of the US Ninth Army advance across a rubble-strewn road as they enter Duisburg, the centre of the Ruhr's industry.

29 MARCH–4 APRIL 1945

THE RUHR ENCIRCLEMENT

KEY

Front line 29 March
Front line 1 April
Front line 4 April

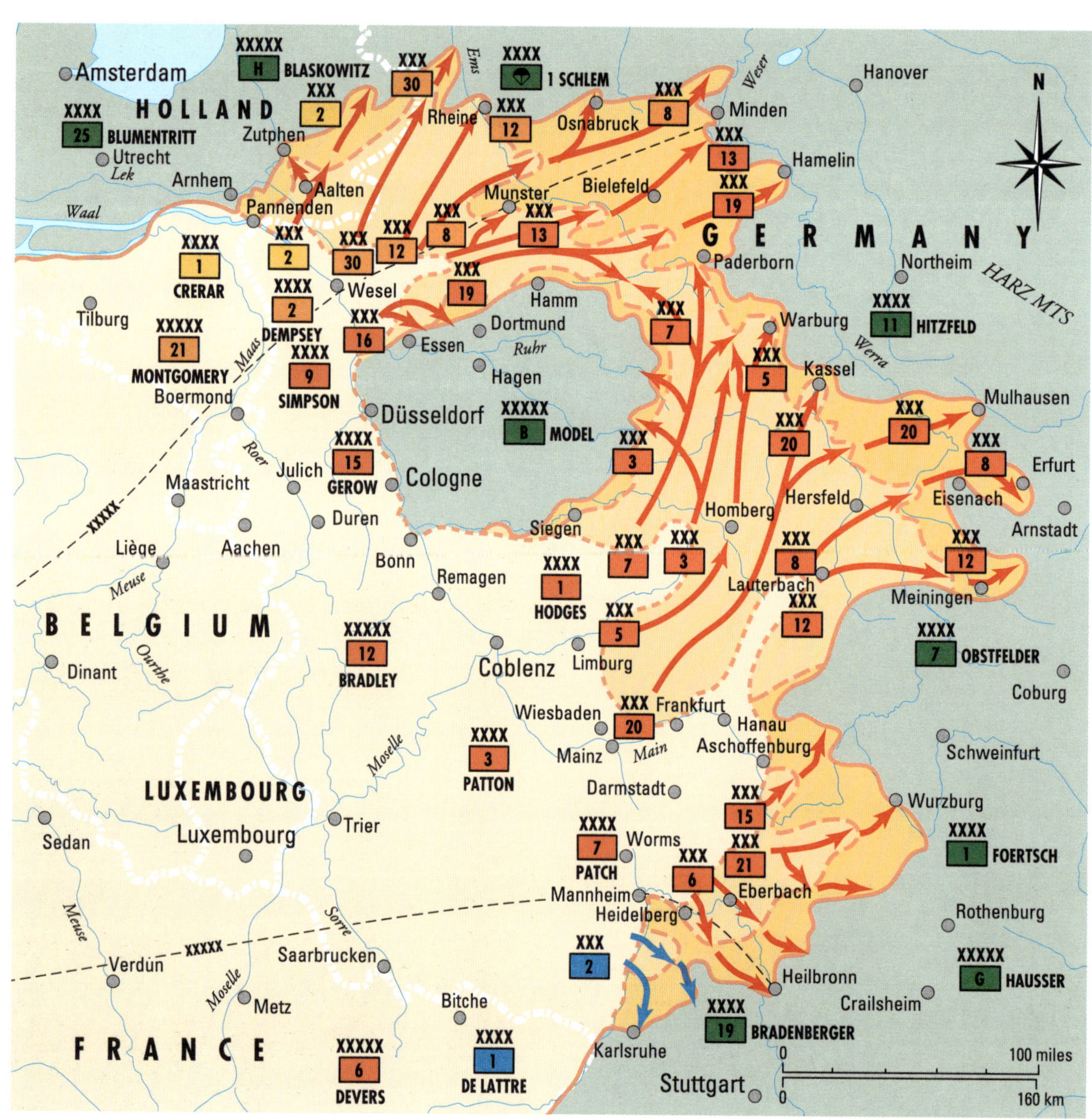

LEFT The Krupp works in Essen, taken by RAF photo reconnaissance aircraft before its capture.

ABOVE US 3rd Armored Division badge.

Paderborn. This delayed Hodges's leading division (3rd Armored of "Lightning Joe" Collins's 7th Corps) which was driving hell for leather to beat Ninth Army to the link-up. Simpson's armour racing east along the eastern edge of the Ruhr, established communications with Collins, and together they agreed that Simpson would cut south immediately, while Collins bypassed Paderborn.

Before first light on 1 April, Ninth Army's 2nd Armored Division met First Army's 3rd Armored, trapping all that remained of Army Group B in a pocket 75 miles by 30 miles. Soon the pocket was split in half, and mass surrenders followed. The Americans captured around 323,000 prisoners, including 24 generals, more than the Russians took at Stalingrad.

Field Marshal Model, nicknamed "Hitler's fireman" because he was continually being sent in to sort out military disasters, was not taken. Bitterly critical of Field Marshal Paulus for surrendering at Stalingrad, saying "a Field Marshal does not become a prisoner", he drove to a forest near Dusseldorf and there shot himself.

ABOVE A German nurse helps an American medic treat a wounded SS soldier captured during the battle to reduce the Ruhr.

ABOVE Prisoners by the acre, these 83,000 were captured by US XVIII Airborne Corps. The total bag of 317,000 was more than twice the estimated number of German troops trapped in the Ruhr.

ALLEZ LA FRANCE!

SUNDAY 19 NOVEMBER 1944–FRIDAY 4 MAY 1945

In the afternoon of 23 November 1944, the *Tricolore* flew from the cathedral in Strasbourg, fulfilling a vow made by Leclerc in the *Serment de Koufra*, the oration by Leclerc after he had captured Kufra in the Libyan Desert nearly four years earlier. The liberation of the Alsatian city had been achieved by a brilliant feat of arms by Leclerc's 2nd Armoured Division taking the Germans totally by surprise. By this time, the French First Army had broken through the Belfort gap, leaving a German pocket at Colmar. When Devers moved troops north to support Patton in the Ardennes offensive, Leclerc learned that the Americans considered it might be necessary to withdraw temporarily from Alsace and Strasbourg, which were threatened by a possible German offensive from the Colmar pocket. Both Leclerc and de Lattre violently opposed such a step. Eisenhower's order to thin out troops preparatory to pulling back was met by a "ça non" from de Lattre.

He ordered the indomitable 3rd Algerian Infantry Division to Strasbourg, and it, with the 1st Free French Division and the US VI Corps, stopped the German thrust north out of the Colmar pocket, Operation Nordwind, after two weeks of bitter fighting. The pocket remained, the elimination of which de Lattre saw as the final step in

FRENCH ORDER OF BATTLE

9 FEBRUARY–8 MAY 1945

CORPS

I Corps: Lt Gen Bethouart, succeeded by Lt Gen Valluy
II Corps: Lt Gen Monsabart

DIVISIONS

1st Armoured Division: Maj Gen Sudre
2nd Armoured Division: Maj Gen Leclerc
5th Armoured Division: Maj Gen Schlesser
1st Free French Division: Maj Gen Garbay
2nd Moroccan Infantry Division: Maj Gen Carpentier
3rd Algerian Infantry Division: Maj Gen Guillaume
4th Moroccan Mountain Division: Maj Gen de Hesdin
9th Colonial Infantry Division: Maj Gen Morliere/Valluy
10th Infantry Division: Maj Gen Billotte

LEFT A Moroccan soldier of the First French Army trails a captured Nazi flag in the dust at Mulhouse captured on 22 November to Colonel Caldairou's Combat Command 3.

ABOVE Fighting on the outskirts of Belfort, which fell on 21 November to soldiers of the 2nd Moroccan Infantry Division and 5th Armored Division under Major General Carpentier.

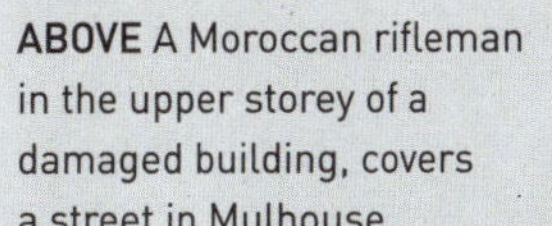

ABOVE A Moroccan rifleman in the upper storey of a damaged building, covers a street in Mulhouse.

ABOVE RIGHT The Croix de Guerre – a French military decoration to reward feats of bravery by individuals or units. The bronze palm indicates that it has been awarded by the Army.

his army's campaign for the liberation of France. In bitter weather, against fanatical German resistance, the pocket was eliminated between 20 January and 9 February by de Lattre's First Army, reinforced by the US XXI Corps.

The American plan was for French First Army to follow US Seventh Army across the Rhine into Germany. De Lattre would not accept this and, after hard fighting, managed to manoeuvre into a position where he had his own crossing point. Although short of river crossing equipment, by a masterpiece of improvisation, French II Corps, commanded by Lieutenant General Joseph de Goislard de Monsabert, out-Pattoned Patton by bouncing the Rhine, between Speyer and Leimersheim, at this point a formidable obstacle fast-flowing and 300 yards wide.

II Corps took Karlsruhe, Pforsheim, and Stuttgart, while I Corps remained on the Rhine covering Strasbourg for a few days, before crossing. In mid April, de Lattre ordered both corps to converge on

MAJOR GENERAL PHILIPPE LECLERC *was the nom de guerre assumed by Captain Viscount Philippe de Hauteclocque to protect his family in France when he joined de Gaulle in England in June 1940. De Gaulle sent him to Chad and, leading French colonial troops, he eventually fought his way north to join the British Eighth Army at Tripoli in January 1943. After fighting in the Tunisian campaign, Leclerc's force became the nucleus of the French 2nd Armoured Division which he led from Normandy to Berchtesgaden.*

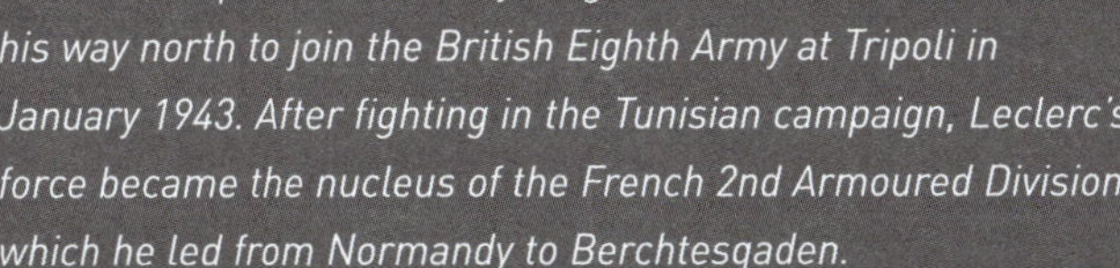

LEFT A tank of the French 2nd Armoured Division drives through Strasbourg's Place Kleber in a liberation parade on 25 November where Major General Leclerc reviewed his victorious soldiers.

ABOVE French 1st Army badge.

LIEUTENANT GENERAL JOSEPH GOISLARD DE MONSABERT *was dashing, fiery and immaculately dressed, served in the First World War, and subsequently in Morocco with de Lattre de Tassigny. He was commanding 3rd Algerian Infantry Division in North Africa in 1942, and in November 1943 his division formed part of General Juin's French Expeditionary Corps in Italy, where he took part in the epic French attack on the Belvedere at Cassino. In July Monsabert's division joined de Lattre's Armée B. On 31 August he became commander II Corps.*

ABOVE French soldiers hand sweets to US soldiers in a jeep in celebration of the closing of the Colmar pocket.

Freudenstadt. I Corps crossed the Danube on 21 April with great *élan*, and by 24 April French troops entered Ulm and reached the shores of Lake Constance. On 4 May, Leclerc's 2nd Armoured Division with US 101st Airborne Division took Hitler's mountain retreat at Berchtesgaden after a lightning dash from Augsburg, while the 3rd Division of US XV Corps approached from the north-east.

By the time the Germans surrendered, nine French divisions were in Germany. First Army had liberated nearly a third of France, and in battle against two German armies had taken quarter of a million prisoners.

ABOVE Soldiers of the 2nd Battalion, 4th Tunisian Tirailleurs enter Scheibenhardt, the first village in Germany to be conquered by the French on 19 March 1945.

LEFT French troops take advantage of the cover afforded by the shallow trench made by tank tracks during clearing operations north of Strasbourg after the elimination of the Colmar pocket in early February.

14 SEPTEMBER 1944–7 MAY 1945

THE FRENCH ADVANCE

KEY

- Front line 14 September 1944
- Front line 20 January 1945
- Front line 9 February 1945
- Front line 19 April 1945
- Front line 7 May 1945

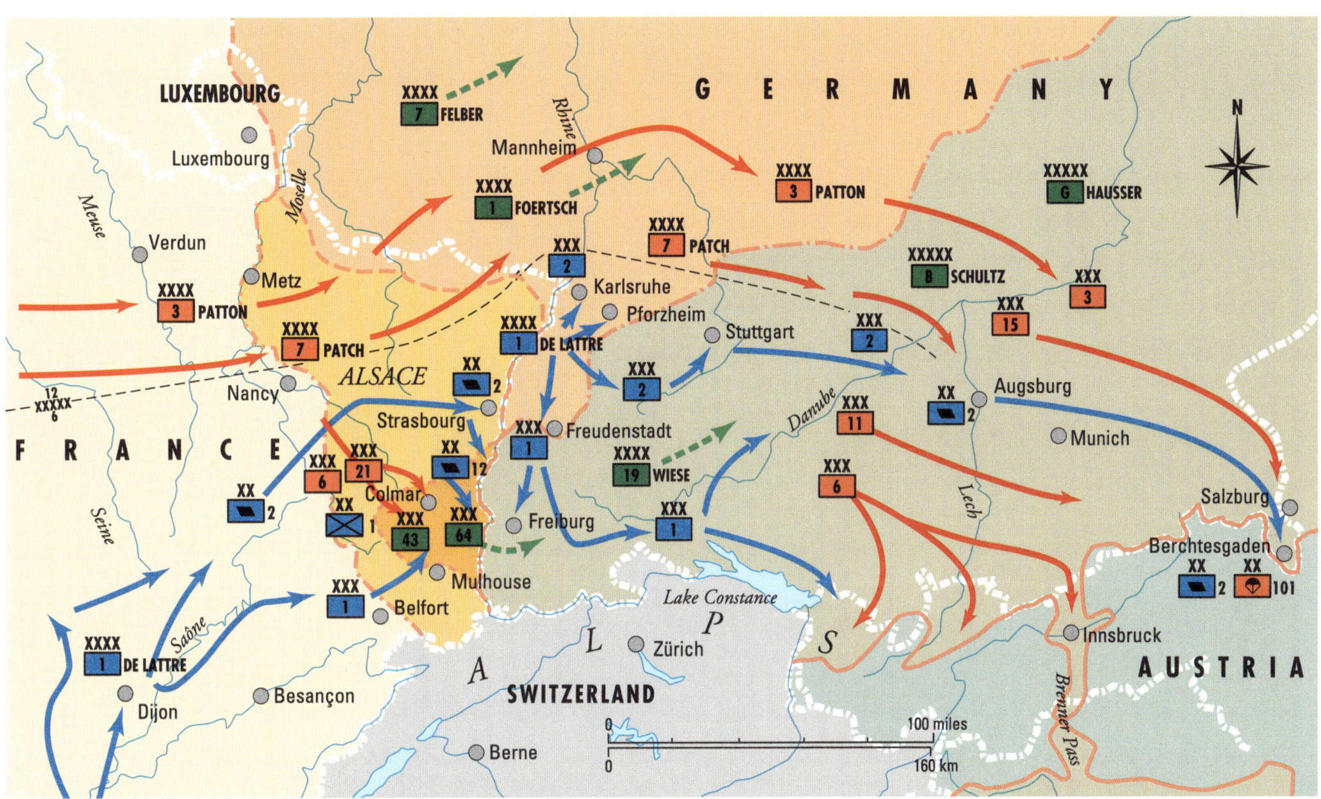

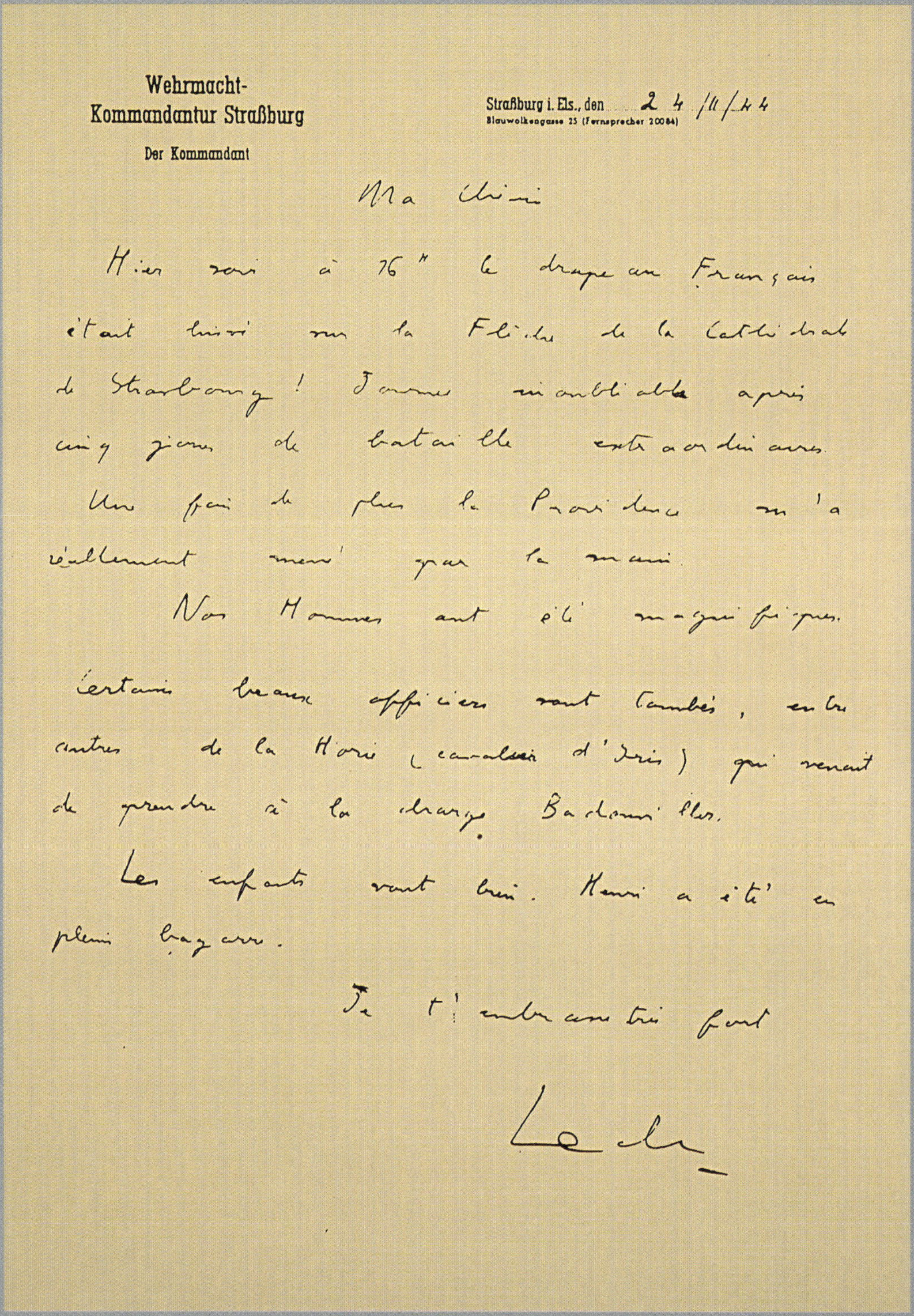

Wehrmacht-
Kommandantur Straßburg
Der Kommandant

Straßburg i. Els., den 24/11/44
Blauwolkengasse 25 (Fernsprecher 20084)

Ma Chérie

Hier soir à 16 h le drapeau Français était hissé sur la Flèche de la Cathédrale de Strasbourg ! Journée inoubliable après cinq jours de bataille extraordinaires.

Une fois de plus la Providence m'a réellement mené par la main.

Nos Hommes ont été magnifiques.

Certains braves officiers sont tombés, entre autres de la Horie (cavalerie d'Iris) qui venait de prendre à la charge Badonviller.

Les enfants vont bien. Henri a été en plein bagarre.

Je t'embrasse très fort

Leclerc

LEFT Major General Leclerc, commanding the French 2nd Armoured Division, had vowed in the African desert in 1941 that he would raise the *Tricolore* over Strasbourg Cathedral. This letter to his wife, written on notepaper taken from the recently captured German headquarters, tells how he fulfilled this vow on 24 November 1944. See translation on page 156.

BELOW Extremely rare propaganda leaflet fired in a propaganda shell by French collaborators on Free French Forces fighting with the Americans in the Vosges region of south-east France in November 1944. It encourages the Free French not to fight with the Americans. See translation on page 156.

«COMME CHEZ SOI»

Un correspondant de guerre américain cable à New-York les détails suivants sur la vie que mènent les soldats américains à Paris.

«Une ou deux fois par semaine, les soldats sont amenés à une représentation dans un cabaret ou un dancing.

«Il arrive naturellement que les soldats aient envie d'organiser une surprise-party. Mais une soirée sans femme n'est pas agréable. On y remédie en téléphonant au Comité et en lui demandant 20 ou 30 jeunes filles. On va les prendre en voiture et, naturellement, on les ramène chez elles en voiture. Du coup, la soirée en est égayée.

«Un soldat allié peut choisir son accompagnatrice pour la durée de son séjour à Paris. Ici encore, le Comité travaille en liaison avec l'unité. On tient à ce que la jeune fille appartienne à la même classe sociale que le soldat. D'ailleurs, on peut dire sans se tromper que ces jeunes filles appartiennent aux meilleures familles de Paris. Grâce à cette fonction du Comité, le soldat allié se sent comme chez soi à Paris et il n'a plus tant à souffrir de la séparation d'avec sa famille».

Les Américains ont de ces trouvailles . . . !

Mais qu'en pensent les fiancés mobilisés des petites «accompagnatrices»?

BELOW A poster showing Tunisian tirailleurs fighting their way across the German border on 19 March 1945, the same action shown in the photograph on page 108. The announcement by General de Lattre de Tassigny tells the French First Army that this moment marks the point of departure for their new mission. See translation on page 156.

RIGHT Morale-boosting poster publicizing the liberation of Strasbourg. In French and Alsace dialect, the text reads "Out with the Boche!"

THE BOMBING OF GERMANY

In 1939, it was firmly believed by the Royal Air Force (RAF) that heavy bombers had the potential to knock an enemy out of a war through precision strikes on key industrial targets. However, experience showed that daylight bombing was suicidal, while precision strikes by night were impossible. Bomber Command suffered a crisis of confidence only salvaged by the appointment of Air Chief Marshal Sir Arthur Harris as its commander in February 1942. He believed bombing alone could win the war and save Allied lives.

Under Harris, the RAF resorted to large-scale night-time area bombing, while working to improve precision technology with the sole aim of putting bombs on factories not on surrounding housing estates. Techniques employed included a radio positioning fixing device known as "Gee", the H2S airborne radar and Pathfinders flying ahead to mark the target. Despite these, night bombing never achieved "surgical" precision. Cologne cathedral, in the centre of the target area, survived the war after 22 attacks on the City. The US Army Air Force had a similar faith in precision bombing, using aircraft that had a higher service ceiling and heavier defensive armament. German day fighters and anti-aircraft guns still inflicted unacceptable losses. The situation only improved with the widespread use of fuel drop tanks after December 1943, allowing Thunderbolt and Mustang fighters to escort the bombers all the way to the target and back. Even then, in bad weather, 80 per cent of American attacks were carried

LEFT RAF pilots' wings.

AIR CHIEF MARSHAL SIR ARTHUR HARRIS

was Commander-in-Chief of Bomber Command in the RAF from 1942–1945. A fervent apostle of strategic bombing as the way to win the war, he was a strong leader and enjoyed the total confidence of his crews despite their appalling losses. He resented tactical missions in support of the army, deeming them diversions from his main task. Thanks to his drive, Bomber Command missions before and after D-Day played a key role in Allied success in north-west Europe.

BOMBING OF GERMANY

RAF BOMBER COMMAND LOSSES

AIRCREW: 55,564 (51 PER CENT)

(highest loss rate of any British Empire armed forces in the Second World War)

BOMBERS: 8,953

USAAF EIGHTH AIRFORCE LOSSES

AIRCREW: 26,000 (12.4 PER CENT)

(highest loss rate of any of the US armed forces in the Second World War)

GERMAN LOSSES

Over 600,000 Germans were killed by bombing

ABOVE The rear gun-turret was a prime target for German nightfighters. This Stirling had been flown by RNZAF Pilot Officer Buck, aged 19. It was his last op.

ABOVE The last moments of a USAAF B-24 Liberator after an attack by German fighters over Austria. This aircraft was flying from Italy to bomb river traffic on the River Danube.

out "blind" by "drenching the target". Civilian casualties were often massive, irrespective of whether the RAF or USAAF were delivering the bombs – although some remarkably accurate raids were carried out by both air forces on oil and transportation targets.

All the major cities in Germany were hit by both air forces. Dresden, the subject of much controversy, was memorably hit (not for the first time) over three days in February 1945. It was a legitimate target. The German Army's own statistics listed 127 factories producing military equipment in the city, and Dresden was a major rail centre. It was bombed at Soviet request in a series of raids on communication centres in eastern Germany, to hinder troops moving to counter the forthcoming Red Army offensive on the Oder.

ABOVE 551 Squadron, 385th Bomb group, USAAF badge.

LEFT The cathedral in Cologne survives. The Hohenzollern bridge was blown by Germans holding the east bank of the Rhine.

TOP A ration pack issued to USAAF aircrew on bombing missions over Germany.

RIGHT Eight USAAF badge.

BELOW Laying out and identifying the dead in Dresden.

LEFT B-17 Flying Fortresses daylight bombing in formation.

The USAAF attack planned for noon on 13 February 1945, before the RAF raid was cancelled because of bad weather. The RAF attacked on the night 13–14 February, followed by the USAAF on the 14th and again on the 15th. Air Chief Marshal Harris, Commander-in-Chief RAF Bomber Command, usually blamed for bombing Dresden, had no power to order a USAAF mission.

Bombing alone did not win the war. It did give a vital contribution in three ways. First, the Luftwaffe lost substantial numbers of aircraft and pilots in battles over Germany against escorted US bombing raids in early 1944, which directly contributed to Allied air superiority throughout the 1944-45 campaign in Europe. Second, the bombing of transportation targets in 1944 and afterwards, such as the railway yards at Dresden, significantly disrupted the German war economy. Third, the Germans expended considerable resources to defend against the bombing. In air defence, Germany deployed 8,876 of their 88-mm guns, as effective against tanks as against aircraft, along with 25,000 smaller flak guns. The flak regiments needed some 900,000 fit men (Rommel only had 500,00 to defend Normandy). Another million men were employed clearing up and repairing bomb damage. Finally, German aircraft production was almost completely concentrated on the production of fighters, especially night fighters, at the expense of long-range bombers and fighter-bombers that could have attacked the Allied armies in the field.

LIEUTENANT GENERAL CARL SPAATZ *took the Eighth United States Army Air Force to England in August 1942, before becoming Allied Air Forces commander under Eisenhower in the Mediterranean. In December 1943 he became Commander-in-Chief of the US Strategic Air Forces (Eighth and Fifteenth air forces). He employed long-range fighters to bring the Luftwaffe to battle and gain air superiority for his daylight bombing missions, specially those against oil targets, which were a major factor in speeding Germany's defeat.*

BELOW Flak concentration map (shown by shaded areas) used by navigator Harry E. Peltzer of the USAAF.

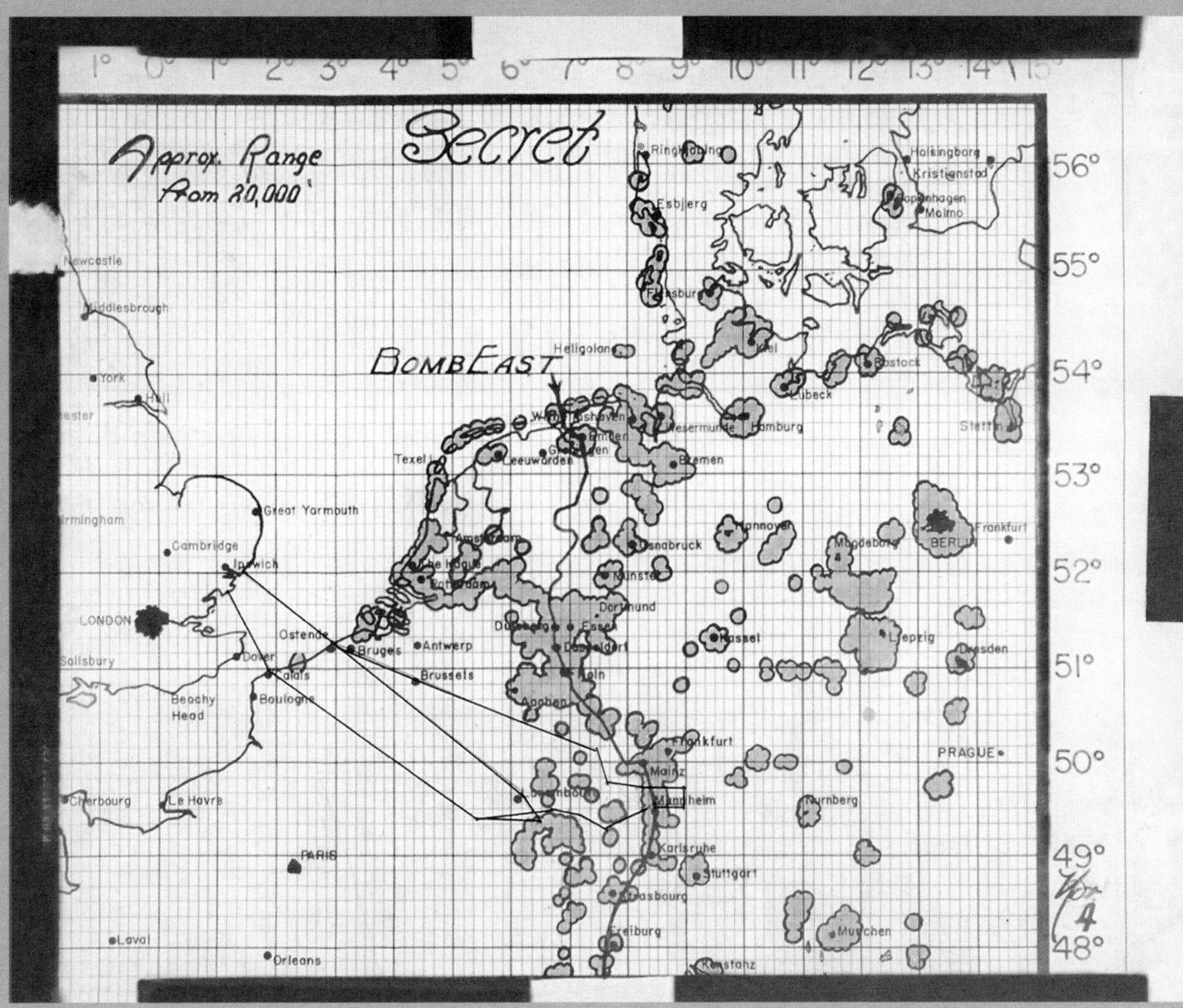

(25) 5 Nov. 44

I.G. Farben Factory - Ludwigshaven

Hit in 3 Engines over the Target - Unable to Feather #1, hit in hub.
Landed near Brussels at a Spit fire Field, almost lost #1 prop, was
biting into the cowling.
Had about 1½ engines on Landing

BELOW Navigational chart for a raid on Gelsenkirchen by RAF's No. 5 Squadron on 5 March 1945, prepared by one of the squadron's navigators, Flying Officer J. W. K. Matthews.

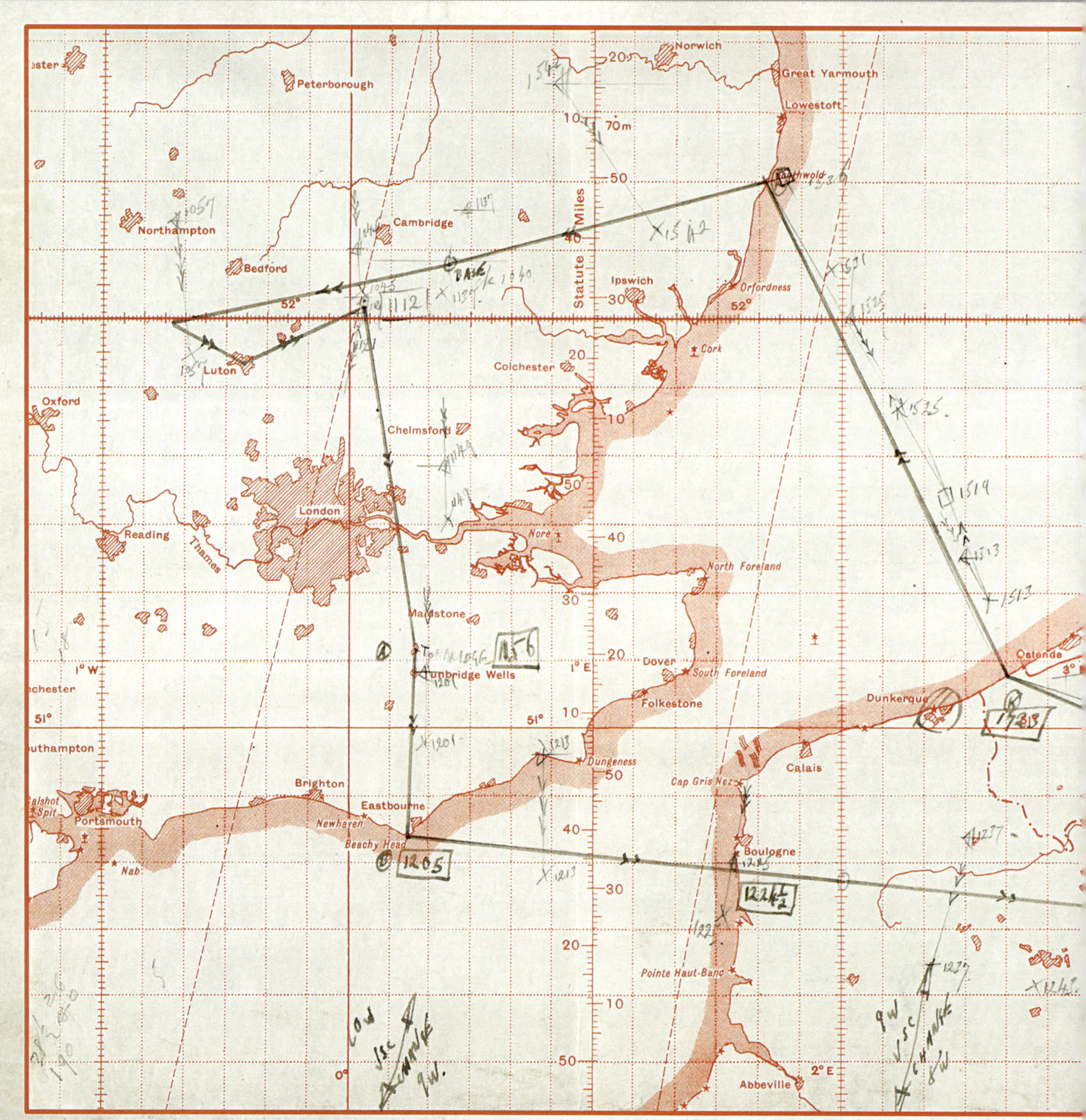

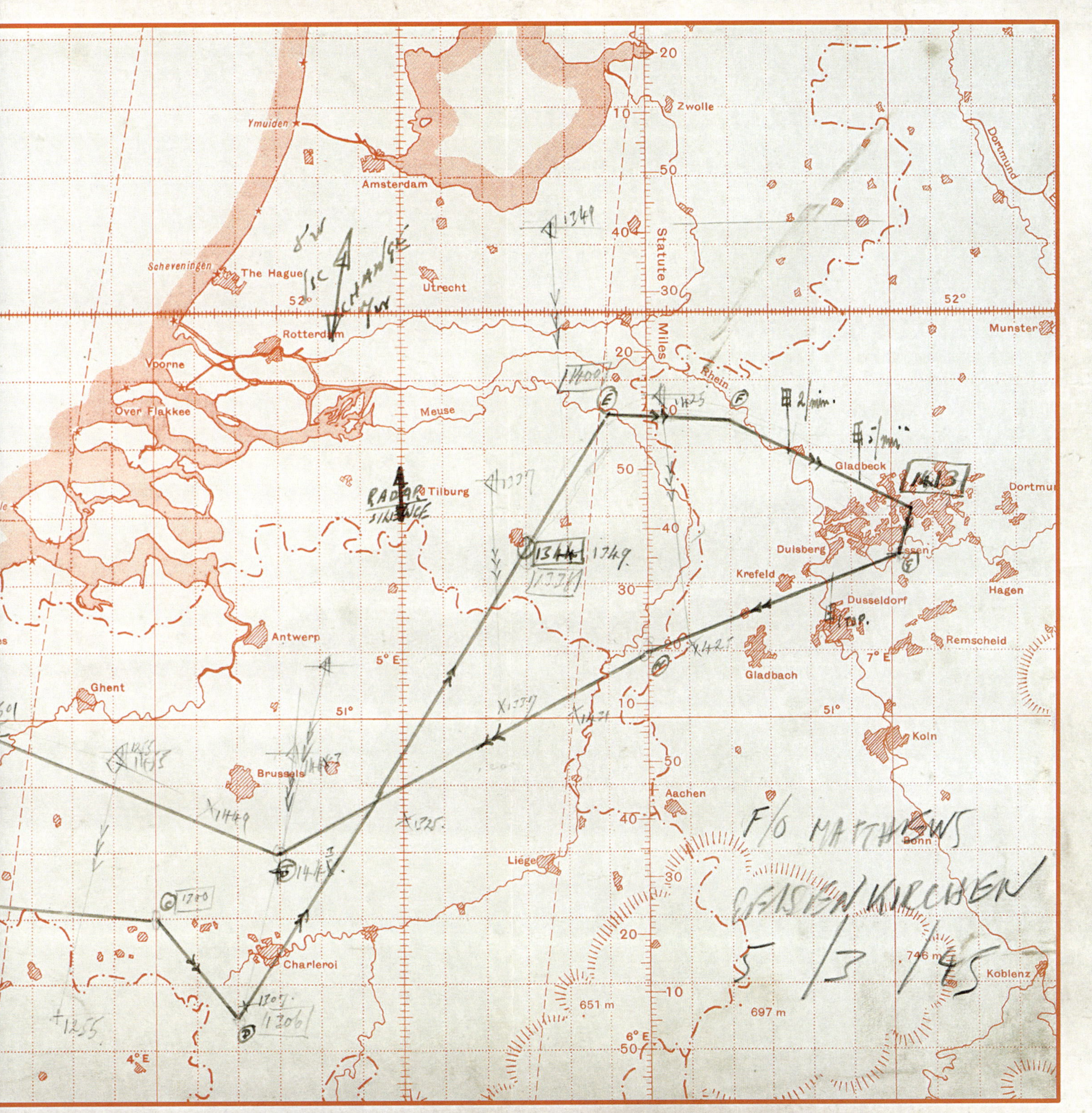

Zwolle
Ymuiden
Amsterdam
Dortmund
Scheveningen
The Hague
Utrecht
Statute Miles
52°
Rotterdam
Munster
Voorne
Rhein
Over Flakkee
Meuse
Gladbeck
Tilburg
Dortmund
RADAR SILENCE
Duisberg
Essen
Krefeld
Hagen
Dusseldorf
Antwerp
Remscheid
5° E
7° E
Gladbach
Ghent
51°
Koln
Brussels
Aachen
F/O MATTHEWS
Bonn
Liege
GELSENKIRCHEN
5/3/45
Charleroi
Koblenz
651 m
697 m
746 m
6° E
4° E

BELOW AND OPPOSITE Personal diary of Lieutenant Burton Gelbman, a 21-year-old USAAF pilot from 385th Bomb Group, with detailed accounts of all his missions in 1944 and 1945. This page recounts details of raids on Mainz and Magdeburg, during which bombs became stuck in the bomb bays, and his plane was attacked by ME-109s and FW-190s. Gelbman started his diary in mid-1944, and continued a day-by-day account of 1945 on the pages designed for the first months of 1944.

Property of Lt. Burton Gelbman
0-775000

In case something happens to me I hereby request that this diary be forwarded to my parents @ 20 Wolffe St. Yonkers (5) New York.

Burton Gelbman
2nd Lt. A.C.

No. 5135½ /86

2700 GALS
#7 MISSION
6HR 50 MIN

JANUARY 13

5x1000 GP
MARSHALLING YDS.
MAINZ

Awoke this AM for 5:50 briefing. Took off at 0805 and climbed to ass. Alt 15,000 ft. Flew in lead sq. Saw some flak on way to IP but, we received no hits. At IP the bomb bay doors wouldn't open. The engineer had to crank them open and closed. After bombs away one bomb stuck in rack bus, after pushing the salvo switch it came loose. Returned to the field to find very poor visibility and the ceiling about 200 ft. We saw the runway and cut our throttles. Luckily we managed to get down okay. Squadron returned without any losses. Bombing P.F.F. with no results.

Full tokyos
#8 MISSION
7HRS 30MIN

JANUARY 14

20x250 GP
OIL REF.
MAGDEBURG

Briefed as usual and formed over the buncher. Flew the Golden Goose again. #3 engine acted up again. When we got near Helgoland in the upper area [illegible] the North Sea. Our upper turret went out of commission. After crossing over land we were attacked by fighters. ME 109's and FW-190. A ship lagging behind our formation was downed. They made one pass at our group and P51's chased them off. The rest of the mission was uneventful and we returned to the base with only a few flak holes from over the target. Bombing was not good.

2780 GALS
10HRS

JANUARY 15

20x250
DESSAU

Awoke for briefing at the usual time the mission to be to Dessau near Berlin. After assembling over the buncher we departed for target. The trip in being uneventful and we flying #6 in the low squadron. Over the target a few rockets were seen and we bombed P.F.F. Clouds of black smoke could be seen coming up from under the undercast so we believe that we hit the target. On the way out the leader got 25 miles off course to the North and we hit flak. We got a few holes one in the left wing and one through the left cockpit window. Upon returning to the field

JANUARY 16

we were told to divert to an R.A.F. base about 115 miles from here about that time we started running around as we were down to less than 200 gal. When we reached the buncher at the [illegible] field [illegible] we let down through the [illegible] that extended from 7,000 to 800 ft. When we broke through. We started looking for the field. The gas was getting very low since the nav (a fellow on his first mission) wasn't sure of the location of the field. We spotted a field and figured we could make it. [illegible] we were supposed to be at [illegible]

SPECIAL DATES TO REMEMBER

1945

JANUARY
1 MISSION SCRUBBED
5. ABORTED #1 ENG OUT
FIFTH MISS. 6 MARSHALLING YDS. SOUTH OF WORMS
7 SIXTH MISSION MARSHALLING YDS - HAMN
13 SEVENTH MISSION " " MAINZ
14 EIGTH " OIL REF MAGDNABURG
16 NINTH " DESSAU
20 TENTH " Heilberron MARSHALLING YD
29 ELEVENTH " ~~Castle~~ Kassel "
30 MISSION SCRUBBED

FEBRUARY
1 RAILWAY YDS AT Wessel 12 MISSION
3 BERLIN 13TH MISSION
6 CHEMNITZ 14TH MISSION OIL PLANT.
9 DUIMAN 15TH MISSION OIL STORAGE
15 RHEINE 16TH MISSION MARSHALLING YDS
17 FRANKFURT 17TH MISSION " "
19 RHEINE 18TH MISSION " "
21 NUREMBURG 19TH " " "
22 BAMBERG 20TH " " "

MARCH
28 KASSEL 21 MISSION " "
7 ULM 22 " " "
8 DORTMUND 23 " MARSHALLING YDS
14 HANNOVER 24 " " "
15 ~~Berlin~~ 25 " " "
ORANIENBURG 26" " "
18 BERLIN 28" " "
19 JENA 27" OPTICAL PLANT
20 HAMBURG 28" MARSHALLING YDS
21 Oldenburg 29 AIRFIELD

MARCH 17

St. Patrick's Day

2700
06
7HRS 45MIN

MARCH 18

18x100 6 INC.
BERLIN

Awoke early for briefing and were briefed for the marshalling yds at Berlin. Went in over Holland and got to Berlin. Heavy Contrails. There were large breaks in the clouds and we bombed visual with good results. The flak was pretty heavy. I received a hit in the windshield which shattered the glass all the way through about an 1" thick. One of our boys Bloom got hit in the bomb bay and the incendiaries caught on fire they bailed out over the target. We returned okay.

BRITISH AND CANADIAN ADVANCES

WEDNESDAY 28 MARCH–THURSDAY 3 MAY 1945

After Montgomery crossed the Rhine with nine British and six American divisions, and three brigades, he planned to advance on Berlin. Eisenhower told him that he was not interested in Berlin: US Ninth Army was to go to Bradley, and Montgomery was to cross the Elbe without delay, drive to the Baltic coast at Lübeck and seal off the Danish peninsula from the possibility of liberation by the advancing Red Army. Somewhat astonished at this change of plan, Montgomery ordered 21st Army Group to reach the line of the Elbe between Hamburg and Wittenburg, and to take Bremen and Hamburg. Canadian First Army was to clear Holland, while the three corps of British Second Army made for the Elbe, severing the German east-west transportation routes, and hooking in to Bremen and Hamburg from the east. The advance began on 28 March 1945.

Across the 300 mile axis of advance lay several waterways before the Elbe was reached: the Dortmund-Ems Canal, the Rivers Weser, Leine, Ems and Aller. Although the Germans were disintegrating, many units put up fierce resistance, inflicting large numbers of casualties on 21st Army Group.

By 8 April, VIII Corps was across the Leine north of Hanover, while XI Corps had reached the Weser, both corps having advanced around 150 miles from the Rhine. On the way, there had been some hard fighting especially at the Dortmund-Ems canal where all the bridges had been blown, as they were over most water obstacles. At Ibbenburen the 3rd Monmouthshires put in repeated attacks on a ridge held by troops from the German NCOs Training School at Hanover. The 5th Batallion Coldstream Guards captured a bridge intact over the Ems at Lingen, found by the Household Cavalry prepared for demolition, and held by three 88 mm guns.

In three weeks, Second Army advanced 200 miles to the Elbe. The engineers had to construct more than 200 bridges, often under fire. Some 78,000 prisoners were taken at the cost of 7,665 casualties.

ABOVE Dutch children on 16 April 1945, after the liberation of Velp by the British 49th Division part of Canadian I Corps. The citizens of Arnhem were forcibly evacuated to Velp.

RIGHT Canadian First Army badge.

By 26 April most of Bremen had been taken, and the next night, the Elbe was crossed with 15th Division and 1st Commando Brigade in the lead. On 29 April, Major General Lyne commanding 7th Armoured Division demanded the surrender of Hamburg, the city capitulated on 3 May to the division that had fought all the way from Alamein.

The Canadian advance through Holland made good progress over difficult terrain interspersed by waterways, such as the Twenthe Canal, strongly held by parachute troops. For operations to clear the Dutch coastline, the II Canadian Corps was greatly assisted by the Polish Armoured Division. As Bremen was being taken, Montgomery ordered the Canadians to seize the German ports of Wilhelmshaven and Emden. At the same time he ordered them not to advance into western Holland, still strongly held, because doing so might cause even greater suffering to the civilian population, many of whom were starving and reduced to eating tulip bulbs to survive.

ABOVE LEFT Soldiers of 1st South Lancashires, 8th Brigade, 3rd Infantry Division, a Normandy assault division, fighting in the railway yards in Bremen which fell on 27 April.

ABOVE Soldiers of 15th Scottish Division with armour and half-tracks waiting for engineers to bridge a mine crater before advancing to the River Elbe.

ABOVE Tanks of 7th Armoured Division, the Desert Rats, approaching a bridge over the River Elbe on their way to take Hamburg.

RIGHT British 7th Armoured Division badge.

5–18 APRIL 1945

ALLIED ADVANCES

KEY

Front line 5 April
Front line 9 April
Front line 18 April

"Major 'Banger' King of the East Yorks had been blown up on a mine and killed. It was he who recited Henry V on the run-in to the Normandy beaches."

LIEUTENANT SYDNEY ROSENBAUM, ROYAL ARTILLERY

LEFT Three of the 14 U-boats found by British troops on the slips in Hamburg's damaged shipyards.

RIGHT A Sherman Firelfly, the British modification to the American Sherman with the 17-pounder gun a vast improvement to the standard 75mm. Fireflies were normally issued on a scale of two per troop, and were quite effective.

BELOW RIGHT Infantry pushes forwards through Bremen past the burning ruins of buildings.

SERGEANT AUBREY COSENS VC *took command of the four survivors of 16 Platoon, D Company, 1st Battalion Queen's Own Rifles of Canada at Mooshof, Holland on the night 25–26 February 1945. They gave him covering fire while he ran forwards to a tank to direct its fire from an exposed position in front of its turret. When a further counter-attack had been repulsed, and on his orders the tank had rammed some farm buildings, he went in alone, killing some of the defenders, and taking the rest prisoner. He did the same in two more buildings but was killed by a sniper soon after.*

THE CONCENTRATION CAMPS

On 4 April, at Ohrdruf, the 4th Armored Division of Patton's Third Army found the first concentration camp discovered by the Western Allies. Although small, Ohrdruf was a foretaste of the horrors yet to be revealed. Patton vomited when he saw it. General Walker, XX Corps commander, forced the burgomaster of Ohrdruf and his wife to tour the camp; afterwards they went home and hanged themselves.

On 11 April, 4th Armored discovered Buchenwald, one of the largest concentration camps. This place was additionally horrible because the former commandant's wife, Ilse Koch, used the tattooed skin of inmates to make lampshades. Also on 11 April, 3rd Armored and 104th Infantry Divisions of US First Army uncovered grisly evidence at Nordhausen. In the dark rooms, prisoners eaten away by diarrhoea and malnutrion lay in filth. Nearby, the Americans found huge underground factories, one for manufacturing V-2 rockets. Near the factory was a slave labour camp, built to hold 30,000 workers. It was clear that no workers left the camp or factory alive, when they became too weak to work; they were left to die, and were cremated, at a rate of 150 a day.

On 15 April, when 11th Armoured Division arrived at Belsen, it was the turn of the British to witness the monstrous cruelties wrought by the Nazis. In the main camp, designed for 8,000 people, there were over 40,000, many dying from deliberate starvation. There had been no food or water in the camp for four days, and typhus and typhoid were raging. About 10,000 unburied bodies lay about the camp. At the far end there were open pits, containing thousands of bodies in varying stages of decomposition. Some 34,000 had died there between February and mid April, and another 13,000 were to die by June, despite the efforts of the Royal Army Medical Corps and volunteers such as British medical students.

The last major camp liberated by the Americans was Dachau on 29 April. Overcome with joy, some of the survivors charged the electric wire and died in their moment of freedom. Others hunted down the guards and beat them to death with anything that came to hand.

CONCENTRATION CAMPS

KEY
(A) Liberators
(B) Estimated Murdered (MINIMUM)

BERGEN-BELSEN (HOLDING CAMP)
(A) British
(B) 70,000 (a further 28,000 died after liberation)

BUCHENWALD (FORCED LABOUR CAMP)
(A) US
(B) 85,000

DACHAU (FORCED LABOUR CAMP)
(A) US
(B) 30,000

DORA-NORDHAUSEN (FORCED LABOUR CAMP)
(A) US
(B) 20,000

FLOSSENBURG (FORCED LABOUR CAMP)
(A) US
(B) 30,000

MAUTHAUSEN (FORCED LABOUR CAMP)
(A) US
(B) 100,000

NEUENGAMME (FORCED LABOUR CAMP)
(A) US
(B) 55,000

Months earlier, thousands of prisoners suffered as a result of frantic efforts by the SS to move them into the middle of Germany in the face of the Russian advance. At least 15,000 died or were shot on forced marches. Weak prisoners were singled out and killed by being injected or gassed. Around 7,000 prisoners were put on ships off Lübeck, which were attacked and sunk in error by British aircraft, thinking they contained soldiers. This was one of the worst maritime disasters in history.

It is estimated that some 600,000 prisoners died in the concentration camps found by the British and Americans. This figure excludes more than six million who were shot in the USSR, died in ghettos, and in Auschwitz, Birkenau, Chelmno, Treblinka, Majdanek, and the other eastern extermination camps of the "final solution".

ABOVE American liberators of the 45th Division at Dachau concentration camp on 29 April 1945.

JOSEF KRAMER, BELSEN COMMANDANT,

was trained at Auschwitz and served at Mauthausen, Dachau and Auschwitz. In late 1944, Kramer was transferred to Belsen, which was enlarged to serve as a convalescent camp for displaced persons from the whole of north-west Europe. There were no gas chambers, but the regime, inaugurated by Kramer, earned him the title "The Beast of Belsen". Corpses rotted in the barracks and rats attacked living victims. Kramer was tried by a British military court and executed in December 1945.

TOP LEFT Inmates of Dachau greet the American liberators of the 45th Division on 29 April 1945. SS troops opened fire as American troops approached the main entrance. The SS were all instantly shot.

OPPOSITE German civilians were brought from Weimar to see the horrors of Buchenwald concentration camp, and were marched through by American military policemen.

ABOVE On 18 April 1945, at the camp of Bergen-Belsen, which had been liberated by the British Army a few days earlier, the burial of the bodies began. Former staff members of the camp, now prisoners of the British Army, were made to bury the bodies of inmates with their bare hands, exposing them to diseases including typhus.

ABOVE The boots of dead inmates were collected and used for fuel by the living at Belsen.

ABOVE Belsen under British guard. SS troops lift bodies on to trucks to take them to the grave pits.

RIGHT Chilling and graphic account of first impression of the Belsen concentration camp, written by Major Hugh Stewart, who commanded the British Army's No. 5 Army Film and Photographic Section. Major Stewart ordered his cameraman to make a detailed record of the scenes of burial and rehabilitation at Belsen.

VISIT to the Concentration Camp at BELSEN

near Celle, Germany, April 19th 1945.

I was taken round this camp by a Major of the RAMC in company with some other officers and War Correspondents. It was my daughter Penelope's sixth birthday.

We drew up outside a building which was part of the barracks of the camp and there saw several hundreds of the prisoners wandering about in a listless sort of way. Many of them looked in bad health and nearly all were too thin, but they were the most healthy of the main camp who had been segregated as quickly as possible to prevent them getting sicker than they were. There were a large proportion of Poles and Jews but they were of all nationalities. A Frenchman who knew English and German well acted as interpreter. One very thin German Jew with his features drawn right in told me he was from the Lipmannstrasse(?) Ghetto in Munich. He said that three men out of half a million were alive from this ghetto and he was one of them. Allowing for exaggeration and possible ignorance of some who might have escaped this still makes a ghastly total. We heard many horrible things from these comparatively well men while we were waiting to be dusted with anti-louse powder. I saw boys of not more than ten years old among the crowds. Those of our party whose anti-typhus inoculations were incomplete were dealt with at once and we all set off to the main part of the camp. My information is that it contains about 60,000 people and is divided into about six sections of which the largest holds 15,000 women. These numbers were not so great until recently but the allied advances have caused several groups of prisoners to be sent there in addition to the normal strength. Prisoners seem to be there for all sorts of reasons, a very large number for no other reason than that they were Jews or Poles. The Frenchman was in for espionage. One professor said something rude about Hitler. I know there were Germans, Poles, Russians, French, Italians, Hungarians and other nationalities. The facts will be published elsewhere, but there were men, women and children of all nationalities, of all ages, of all stages of illness until death itself and corpses dead for weeks and possibly months. So much for the general picture. To continue with the description of my visit.

The first thing I remember were groups of ragged dejected looking people behind barbed wire which had been broken down in most places. Blocks of one storey buildings appeared to be the only accommodation but I did not enter any till later. Suddenly I was conscious of the most appalling stench: the wind was blowing into my face. I could not see what caused the stench although I began to notice odd dead bodies lying around and nobody seemed to worry about it. As we went on further I saw a group of about 20 bodies with their clothes off- men women and children- just dumped in a pile. Live prisoners were squatting or walking near them quite unconcerned. Then I noticed something that was a further stage in degradation. Men and women performed their elementary needs of the body quite shamelessly out in the open and all muddled up. One of my officers told me he saw a woman use a corpse as something to sit on while she relieved her Dysentery and I can well believe it. They got up without any attempt to wipe their posteriors. Every one was pale and haggard beyond belief. Most of the corpses appeared to have died from hunger. Their limbs were like my wrist and their skin looked like rubber stretched over skeleton. They were discoloured in varying stages of decay and still the live ones carried on their existences as though they were not there at all.

After a short time we came on a pile of dead female bodies, 80 yards by 30 yards, and about 3 feet high. There must have been at least 500 lying there thrown on top of one another so thin and so emaciated it was difficult to believe they had ever been people at all. Many of them were covered in horrible sores. The sight was something that I am quite unable to describe and the smell was its equal. And yet even here there were people sitting down cooking a potato on a fire or lying in the sun.

THE ELBE AND THE EAGLE'S NEST

WEDNESDAY 11 APRIL–FRIDAY 4 MAY 1945

On 4 April Bradley's 12th Army Group launched the new Allied main effort, aimed at splitting Germany by linking with the Red Army. While the new Fifteenth Army held the Rhine's west bank opposite the Ruhr and began occupation duties, Hodges' First Army headed east to Leipzig. Patton's Third Army was to head for Chemnitz, but be prepared to swing south to help Devers's Sixth Army Group's advance into Southern Germany. Simpson's Ninth Army aimed for the Elbe near Magdeburg, from where roads led to Berlin. Simpson was under the impression that Berlin was his army's objective – Bradley had told him as much.

By nightfall on 6 April, First and Ninth Armies were across and heading away from the River Weser, while Patton, let off the leash by Bradley, raced ahead towards Weimar. Two of Simpson's divisions had their eyes firmly fixed on the Elbe and Berlin; the 2nd Armored, and 83rd Infantry, whose collection of "liberated" enemy and civilian vehicles earned them the name the "Rag Tag Circus".

ABOVE Ninth Army infantrymen fire against snipers in Tangemunde, Germany, during the battle for the Elbe River town. The last water barrier before Berlin, the Elbe was crossed on 14 April 1945 by Ninth Army troops.

LEFT Smoke from burning buildings darken the sky as the 30th Infantry Division of the US Ninth Army assaults Born, 23 miles north of Magdeburg in the drive to the Elbe.

"Everyone and his brother are trying to get into town."

101ST AIRBORNE MESSAGE ON RACE TO GET TO BERCHTESGADEN

2ND LIEUTENANT WILLIAM D. ROBERTSON, *the 1st battalion intelligence officer, was heading for Torgau on 25 April 1945, as patrols from the 273rd Infantry, 69th Division were pushing forwards to contact the Russians on the Elbe. Hearing firing, he found some paint in a shop in Torgau, and painted a crude American flag on a table cloth. Clutching the flag, he scrambled over the twisted girders of the wrecked railway bridge over the Elbe. About halfway across, a Russian solder climbing towards him met him. It was 4.00 p.m.*

ABOVE Infantrymen of Hodges's US First Army greet Russians of Marshal Koniev's First Ukrainian Army on a demolished bridge over the Elbe at Torgau.

In the late afternoon of 11 April, leading elements of 2nd Armored dashed for a bridge over the Elbe just south-east of Magdeburg, but found it demolished. Disappointed but euphoric, they had covered 73 miles that day – Berlin was only 70 miles away. The "Rag Tag Circus" was not far behind, and the next day crossed the Elbe in assault boats. Simpson had a crossing. That day Roosevelt died, and Vice President Truman became president.

As the Americans closed up to the Elbe, the Russians were still on the Oder, and had not yet entered what was to be the Soviet zone of occupation. Simpson was confident that given two days to re-supply, he could be in Berlin in 24 hours, beating the Russians who had not yet started their offensive. Simpson flew to Bradley's headquarters to present his plan "to enlarge the Elbe River bridgehead to include Potsdam". Bradley telephoned Eisenhower, to be told there would be

LEFT Americans and Russians in Torgau after the link-up on the River Elbe where patrols of the US 273rd Infantry and Russian 173rd Infantry Regiment met.

TOP US 69th Infantry Division badge.

MAJOR GENERAL MAXWELL TAYLOR

became the first American general to fight in France in the Second World War when he dropped with his 101st Airborne Division in Normandy on D-Day. His division, the "Screaming Eagles", after their shoulder patch, made a major contribution to the success of Overlord. With the 82nd, Taylor's division played a major role in Market Garden, and stayed fighting in Holland for two months afterwards. To his chagrin, Taylor missed the fighting at Bastogne, being on leave in the USA. His division was among the first to get into Berchtesgaden.

ABOVE Privates Constable and Bryan, and Corporals Shumaker and Goodney of the US 5th Tank Destroyer Group relax and enjoy Hitler's favourite view on the terrace of mountain home in Bavaria.

no drive on Berlin. Eisenhower's decision to halt the American armies on the Elbe, was not for lack of supplies, or because of the Germans, but in order to save casualties while taking what he regarded as a mere prestige objective.

As the First and Ninth Armies breasted up to the Elbe to await the arrival of the Russians, Patton's Third and Patch's Seventh Armies vied to be first into the "National Redoubt", in the vicinity of Salzburg and Berchtesgaden, where misleading intelligence led the Allies to believe the Nazi last stand would be staged. In the end it was congestion not resistance that slowed the competition to be the first to get to Berchtesgaden, The race was between the US 3rd Division of General Patch's Seventh Army, and the US 101st Airborne slogging up the road on their feet, supported by the dashing troopers of Leclerc's French 2nd Armored. Late in the afternoon of 4 May, motorized elements of 3rd Division pipped them to the post – just. There was no Nazi last stand.

LEFT American and French soldiers stand in the picture window of Hitler's living room. Here the German leader treated his cronies to interminable diatribes over cream cakes and tea.

19 APRIL–7 MAY 1945

ALLIED ADVANCES

KEY

- Front line 19 April
- Front line 25 April
- Front line 7 May

HITLER'S LAST DAYS

SUNDAY 1 APRIL–WEDNESDAY 2 MAY 1945

On 1 April 1945, to avoid the disruption caused by air raids, Hitler moved from his quarters in the new Reich Chancellery in Berlin to the Führerbunker just behind the chancellery building. Here the remnants of his "court" assembled, in an unreal atmosphere of refusal to acknowledge that nothing could save the Third Reich.

Communications in the bunker were so poor that senior staff officers had to trail up from the Armed Forces' High Command bunkers at Zossen, 15 miles south of Berlin, twice a day for briefings; hardly an effective command system. Hitler's decision to remain in Berlin, and not move to Zossen where he could have commanded more efficiently, was a symptom of his descent into fantasy.

The Soviet Army was on the Oder and Neisse Rivers about 50 miles from Berlin. Stalin had just ordered Marshal Georgi Zhukov's First Belorussian Front, supported by Marshal Ivan Koniev's First Ukrainian Front, to take Berlin. Actually he wanted to see who of the two would get there first. The Wehrmacht facing the Russians had 90 divisions consisting of 10,000 guns, 1,500 tanks, and in Berlin itself, 200,000 men.

Taking huge losses, Zhukov breached the brilliantly organized defences of the Seelow Heights, and the Germans withdrew to the outer ring of Berlin's defences. A raving Hitler, deploying imaginary formations that existed only in his mind, ordered one last effort to throw the Russians back: "Any commander who holds his men back will forfeit his life within five hours". On 22 April, he gave way to despair, ordering his staff to escape, but refusing to do so himself. A handful stayed, most scuttled off, some to die by shell fire, bombing, or at the hands of Russian soldiers fighting their way in to Berlin.

At this point the Nazi regime finally began to unravel. On 23 April, Goering telegraphed Hitler proposing that as he was cut off in Berlin, he, Goering was now the leader of the Reich – temporarily. On 26 April, Hermann Fegelein, Himmler's liaison officer and brother-in-law of Eva Braun, Hitler's companion, was caught preparing to escape from Berlin in civilian clothes. He was arrested and later shot, after Hitler had learned the next day that Himmler had been attempting to cut a secret deal with the Allies.

RIGHT The Russian T-34 first appeared in 1940, with sloped armour, American Christie suspension and broad tracks that were excellent on soft ground and snow. It had a crude finish, but it was also tough, simple, reliable and produced in vast numbers.

HITLER *returned to Berlin unannounced on 15 January 1945, after the failure of the Ardennes offensive. A month later Eva Braun, his companion for 12 years, joined him. After briefly visiting the front in March 1945, Hitler never left Berlin again. Apart from evening strolls with his Alsation dog in the pauses between American daylight and British night time bombing, he only left the bunker briefly to discuss defence plans with officials and commanders and to congratulate members of the Hitler Youth on the award of the Iron Cross.*

"If Goebbels and Bormann do not agree to unconditional surrender, we'll blast Berlin into ruins."

MARSHAL GEORGI ZHUKOV

By now four Soviet Armies (Third, Fifth, Forty-seventh Shock, and 3rd Guards Tank) had broken into the Berlin suburbs. By 25 April, Berlin was split in two and surrounded. In the centre, Wehrmacht and Volksturm resistance was as stubborn as ever, as the Russians chopped the city in to ever-smaller sectors to prevent any concentration of force.

On 28 April Hitler dictated his personal and political testaments, naming Grand Admiral Karl Doenitz as President and Goebbels as Chancellor. On 29 April, Hitler married Eva Braun, and dictated his last will and testament. The next afternoon, with the Russians a mere 400 yards away, he shot himself, while Eva Braun took poison. Their bodies were drenched with fuel and burnt in the Chancellery Garden. Dr Joseph and Magda Goebbels committed suicide after she had administered cyanide to their six children.

ABOVE RIGHT A re-staging of the Red Flag being hoisted over the Reichstag. The 150th Rifle Division claims to have planted a Red Flag on 1 May, but savage fighting continued in the building for another 24 hours.

RIGHT The Chancellery, Berlin, Hitler has emerged from his bunker to congratulate boys of the Hitler Youth on winning the Iron Cross. Here he is speaking to Alfred Czech, a 12-year old.

Outside, the Germans continued a fanatical resistance, fighting house-to-house, floor-by-floor. On 30 April the Soviet flag flew over the Reichstag. The last pockets of resistance in a handful of government buildings fell on 2 May, when Major Vladimirovna Nikulina, a member of a storm detachment, hoisted the Red Flag over Hitler's headquarters. The remnants of the Berlin garrison surrendered at 3.00 p.m. on 2 May.

The savage fighting for Berlin from 16 April–2 May alone cost the Russians 305,000 casualties.

MARSHAL GEORGI ZHUKOV *carried a far greater weight of responsibility than any Western Allied general. A member of the Stavka (the Supreme Command Headquarters), as well as a brilliant field commander, he frequently implemented the battlefield strategy he had had a hand in formulating. His duties were often equivalent to those carried out by Marshall and Eisenhower, or Brooke and Monty. He was a ruthless, fighting soldier, sometimes defying Stalin, but too valuable for even that grisly ogre to dispense with.*

ABOVE LEFT After Hitler's suicide, General Krebs, Chief of General Staff, met Colonel General Chuikov to discuss terms, but was sent away when he would not agree to unconditional surrender. He committed suicide in Hitler's bunker the next day.

ABOVE A scene in Berlin at the end of the war. An elevated bridge carries the U-Bhan. 8th Guards Army tanks can be seen under this bridge at the southern end of the Wilhemstrasse. The canal bridge has been destroyed.

Mein politisches Testament.

Seit ich 1914 als Freiwilliger meine bescheidene Kraft im ersten, dem Reich aufgezwungenen Weltkrieg einsetzte, sind nunmehr über dreissig Jahre vergangen.

In diesen drei Jahrzehnten haben mich bei all meinem Denken, Handeln und Leben nur die Liebe und Treue zu meinem Volk bewegt. Sie gaben mir die Kraft, schwerste Entschlüsse zu fassen, wie sie bisher noch keinem Sterblichen gestellt worden sind. Ich habe meine Zeit, meine Arbeitskraft und meine Gesundheit in diesen drei Jahrzehnten verbraucht.

Es ist unwahr, dass ich oder irgendjemand anderer in Deutschland den Krieg im Jahre

- 2 -

1939 gewollt haben. Er wurde gewollt und angestiftet ausschliesslich von jenen internationalen Staatsmännern, die entweder jüdischer Herkunft waren oder für jüdische Interessen arbeiteten. Ich habe zuviele Angebote zur Rüstungsbeschränkung und Rüstungsbegrenzung gemacht, die die Nachwelt nicht auf alle Ewigkeiten wegzuleugnen vermag, als dass die Verantwortung für den Ausbruch dieses Krieges auf mir lasten könnte. Ich habe weiter nie gewollt, dass nach dem ersten unseligen Weltkrieg ein zweiter gegen England oder gar gegen Amerika entsteht. Es werden Jahrhunderte vergehen, aber aus den Ruinen unserer Städte und Kunstdenkmäler wird sich der Hass gegen das, letzten Endes verantwortliche Volk immer wieder erneuern, dem wir das alles zu verdanken haben: Dem internationalen Judentum und seinen Helfern!

Ich habe noch drei Tage vor Ausbruch des deutsch-polnischen Krieges dem britischen Botschafter in Berlin eine Lösung der deutsch-polnischen Probleme vorgeschlagen – ähnlich der im Falle des Saargebietes unter internationaler Kontrolle. Auch dieses Angebot kann nicht weggeleugnet werden. Es wurde nur

Fernschreibstelle Standarte 13 — Geheim — Geheime Kommandosache

Fernschreibname LNX Laufende Nr. 0446

Angenommen / Aufgenommen — Datum: 30.4.45 — um: 0310 Uhr — von: LBRE — durch: h.

Befördert: Datum: 19 — um: Uhr — an: — durch: — Rolle:

-- G E H E I M -

Fernschreiben

+ FRR MBBS 06274 29.4. 2230.=

An

FRR LDN WISMAR.=

NACH EINGANG G. KDOS BEHANDELN STABSOBERMEISTER GOERE .=

FOLGENDER FUNKSPRUCH IST SOFORT AN WEHRMACHTFUEHRUNGSSTAB NORD ZU UEBER MITTELN. LAUT MITTELUNG HIES. HEERESDIENSTSTELLE VERELGT WFST VON RHEINSBERG IN RICHTUG WISMAR. DORT SOLL BEREITS TEIL WFST SEIN FT UMGEHEND AN ZUSTAENDIGE STELLE UEDERMITTELN: ENTSCHL FUNKSPRUCH VON GRAU 2 A :

'' FRR GEN OBERST JODL ZEPPELIN).-

ES IST MIR SOFORT ZU MELDEN :

1) WO SIND DIE SPITZEN VON '' WENCK''??

2) WANN GREIFEN SIE WEITER AN ?.-

3) WO IST DIE 9. ARMEE?.-

4) WOHIN BRICHT DIE 9. ARMEE DURCH.?.-

5) WO SIND DIE SPITZEN VON '' HOLSTE''?.-

ADOLF HITLER''.-

ANTOWRT SOFORT AN MAR. NACHR. ABTEILUNG DER SEEKRIEGSLEITUNG DURCH FUNK UEBER HEERESFUNKSTELLE PLOEN, FERNSCHREIB UEBER MARINE MBSN MARINE – MBBS – MWHB) NACH PLOEN GEBEN.=

MNA / SKL +

Unterschrift des Aufgebers — Fernsprech-Anschluß des Aufgebers

ABOVE Part of Hitler's Political Testament dictated by the Führer to his secretary Frau Junge shortly after his marriage to Eva Braun, and signed at 4.00 a.m. on the 19 April in the Reich Chancellery bunker. Dr Joseph Goebbels, Martin Bormann, Wilhelm Burgdorf and Hans Krebs also signed as witnesses. See translation on pages 156–57.

LEFT One of Hitler's last secret telegrams from the Reich Chancellery bunker to Colonel General Jodl, sent on the day before Hitler committed suicide. His five staccato questions requesting information on the whereabouts of forces he thought were about to break through the Soviet cordon around the capital read like a desperate call for help. The help never came. The Third Reich ceased to exist nine days later. See translation on pages 156–57.

TO THE BALTIC AND DENMARK

TUESDAY 1 MAY–MONDAY 7 MAY 1945

On 1 May the Russians reached Rostock, barely 35 miles from Wismar, on the shores of the Baltic, and a further 30 to Lübeck. To seal off the whole of the Schleswig peninsula and Denmark from the Russians, Montgomery sent Ridgway's XVIII Airborne Corps, which included the British 6th and US 82nd Airborne Divisions, racing to Wismar.

After a 50-mile drive, the British 6th Airborne Division reached Wismar on 2 May, at the head of XVIII US Airborne Corps. Lieutenant Colonel Napier Crookenden, commanding officer of the British 9th Parachute Battalion, ordered to go forward to make contact with the Red Army, took two Russian-speaking sergeants of the Canadian Parachute Battalion, and a white flag fashioned out of a sheet. Driving east in an open staff car, he encountered Red Army tanks. While speaking to the most senior Soviet officer he could find through his interpreters, he was passed by a stream of tanks roaring off towards Wismar at top speed. Crookenden sprang into his car, hustled the Soviet officer in with him, and after a hair-raising drive, the Russian gripping his arm in a state of panic, he overtook and halted the tanks.

The Soviet officer on being taken to Major General Eric Bols, commanding 6th Airborne, said that his objective was Copenhagen, and that was where he was going. Nothing would dissuade him. Finally Bols turned to the interpreter and said, "tell this fellow I have a complete airborne division and five regiments of guns. If he does not clear off, I will open fire." At this the Russian grinned and became much more co-operative.

BELOW Muzzle flash lights up the sky as 155 mm guns of 8 Battery, 53rd Heavy Regiment Royal Artillery fired for three hours across the Elbe on 30 April 1945.

BELOW Soldiers of British 6th Airborne Division greeting a Russian tank crew in Wismar after the Russian advance on Lubeck had been halted by the Airborne Division's commander.

ABOVE British 6th Airborne Division badge.

ABOVE British armoured cars crossing the Canal Bridge at Kiel on their way to Denmark. They were sent by Field Marshal Montgomery to maintain communications between him General Dewing.

The German capitulation at Lüneburg Heath on 4 May included Denmark, and the Resistance took control of the country the following day. With 2.5 million armed prisoners in 21st Army Group's area of Germany, as well as over two million refugees, Montgomery did not have enough troops to establish order in northern Germany and send substantial forces to occupy Denmark.

On 5 May, he sent Major General Richard Dewing, head of the SHAEF Mission to Denmark, to Copenhagen by air. He took with him a company of the 13th Parachute Battalion of the 6th Airborne Division in 12 C-47 Dakotas, and a strong fighter escort flew top cover. The party landed in Copenhagen at 5.00 p.m. to great rejoicing.

MAJOR GENERAL RICHARD DEWING *served with the Indian Army in Mesopotamia in the First World War. In the Second, he held a number of important senior staff appointments, such as deputy to Field Marshal Sir John Dill, the Head of the British Joint Services Mission in Washington, before heading the Army and Air Liaison Staff in Australia. He was eminently suited to lead the Supreme Headquarters Allied Expeditionary Force Mission to Denmark. He ended his army career on the Allied Control Commission in Berlin.*

GRAND ADMIRAL KARL DOENITZ *was one of the few convinced Nazis among the senior officers in the German Navy. A U-boat commander in the First World War, Hitler chose him to command the U-boats in the Second. Both his sons were lost in U-boats. He succeeded Admiral Erich Raeder as Commander-in-Chief of the Navy on 30 January 1943. After succeeding Hitler, he set up a government at Flensburg. Captured by the British on 22 May 1945, he had been Reich President for 23 days.*

The following day, Montgomery was able to reassure Whitehall, who were, according to him, "belly-aching about Denmark", that all was well. The Germans were keeping to their barracks, and there were no reported violations of the surrender agreement. Montgomery sent in the balance of the 13th Parachute Battalion as a reserve as well as an armoured car regiment. The latter, with good mobility and communications, could keep Dewing thoroughly in the picture as it patrolled over the country.

The one exception to the peaceful picture painted by Montgomery, was the island of Bornholm (80 miles north-east of the mouth of the River Oder), where the garrison consisted of some 20,000 fighting men, including a division that had escaped from Poland with much of its equipment. The German commandant refused to surrender, so on 7 and 8 May, Russian aircraft bombed the towns of Ronne and Neks, causing considerable damage, but fortunately killing few people. On 9 May, Soviet warships arrived at Ronne, and the Germans surrendered. Soviet occupation of Bornholm lasted until April 1946.

TOP General Dewing, Chief of SHAEF Mission, inspecting a parade of soldiers of the underground movement at the airfield.

ABOVE Soldiers of the British 13th Parachute Battalion being greeted in Copenhagen by enthusiastic crowds, wild with joy at being liberated.

NB!

H OD/EM 4.5 20.30 SURRENDER SNAP

Field Marshal MONTGOMERY announces that all German Forces in North-West GERMANY, HOLLAND, and DENMARK have surrendered. The surrender becomes effective at 8 o'clock D.B.S.T. tomorrow morning.

AGENCIES END 3 lines

ABOVE A copy of the telegram confirming the surrender of German forces in north-west Germany, Holland and Denmark. This was read over the air to Danes listening to the BBC on 4 May by Flemming Barfoed, who had once finished second in the hurdles at the Danish championships. "More upcoming in a moment" is written across the bottom of the telegram.

UNCONDITIONAL SURRENDER

THURSDAY 3 MAY–TUESDAY 8 MAY 1945

After Hitler's suicide, Admiral Doenitz, based at Flensburg, who had succeeded to the leadership of the Reich, ordered all his armies to surrender to the western Allies. He hoped to continue resistance to the Russians, and conclude a treaty with the Americans and British. When Admiral Hans von Friedeberg, the new head of the German Navy, appeared at Montgomery's headquarters at Lüneburg Heath on 3 May bearing a surrender offer on those terms, Montgomery sent him back to Field Marshal Keitel, the Chief of German High Command, telling him to think again.

The next day, Friedeberg appeared at Lüneburg, and unconditionally surrendered to Montgomery all German forces in north-west Germany, including those in Holland and Denmark. The surrender became effective on 5 May 1945.

On the same day, Friedeberg, representing Doenitz, arrived at Eisenhower's headquarters at Rheims. On being asked his business by Eisenhower's Chief of Staff, Major General Bedell Smith, it became clear that he had no authority to sign a surrender and that General Jodl was on his way to assist in negotiations. Eisenhower deduced that Doenitz was playing for time, so that he could transfer the largest possible number of German soldiers behind the Western Allied lines. Eisenhower responded by instructing Bedell Smith to tell Jodl that unless they ceased prevaricating, he would prevent any refugees entering Allied lines, by implication, throwing them to the tender mercy of the Soviets.

The unconditional surrender on all fronts was signed by Jodl in the presence of Eisenhower at 2.41 a.m. on 7 May, to become effective at midnight on 8 May 1945. Included in the provisions of the document was the requirement for the German commanders to appear in Berlin at a time set by the Red Army high command to surrender to the Soviet Union.

FIELD MARSHAL WILHELM KEITEL

nicknamed "lakaital" (lackey), was made chief of the high command of the armed forces by Hitler when the Nazi leader assumed supreme command in 1938. Promoted to field marshal after the fall of France, he threatened to resign to discourage Hitler from invading Russia, but stayed on nevertheless. His influence diminished thereafter, although he remained slavishly devoted to Hitler, and was second only to him in directing the war. He was found guilty at Nuremberg and executed on 16 October 1946.

ABOVE Badge of the Supreme Headquarters Allied Expeditionary Forces (SHAEF).

"You should have thought of all of this six years ago."

MONTY RESPONSE TO FRIEDEBURG WHEN HE EXPRESSED CONCERN ABOUT THE GERMAN CIVIL POPULATION.

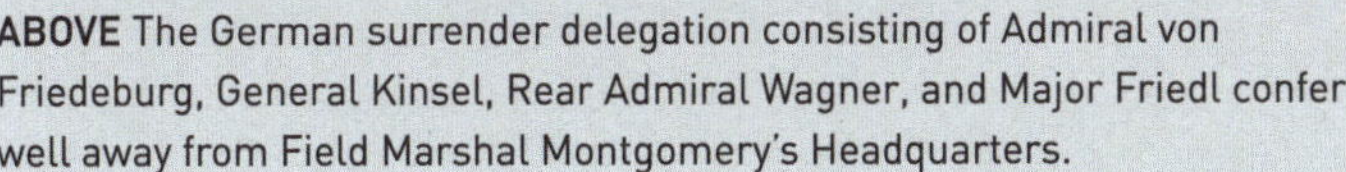

ABOVE The German surrender delegation consisting of Admiral von Friedeburg, General Kinsel, Rear Admiral Wagner, and Major Friedl confer well away from Field Marshal Montgomery's Headquarters.

TOP RIGHT From left to right: Air Chief Marshal Sir Arthur Tedder, deputy to General Eisenhower, Marshal Zhukov, and General Carl Spaatz, commander of the United States Air Forces, toast the signing of the unconditional surrender.

RIGHT General Eisenhower with, on his left, his deputy Air Chief Marshal Sir Arthur Tedder RAF, makes his victory speech to the press in a school house in Rheims.

OPPOSITE General Kinsel, Chief of Staff of the German Army North, signing the surrender terms, watched by Field Marshal Montgomery and Colonel Ewart.

ABOVE General Jodl signs the instrument of surrender at Rheims. On his left Admiral Hans von Friedeburg, and on his right, his ADC Major General Wilhelm Oxonius.

ABOVE Lieutenant General Bedell Smith, Eisenhower's Chief of staff, signs the Surrender Document on behalf of the Allied High Command. On his right Admiral Burrough and on his left Major General Susloparaff.

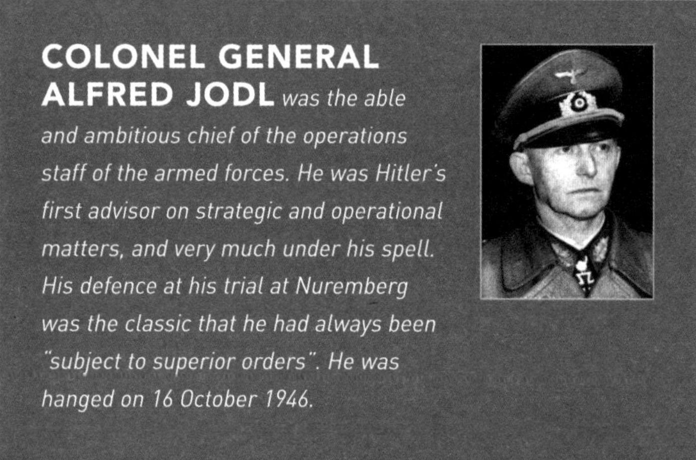

COLONEL GENERAL ALFRED JODL *was the able and ambitious chief of the operations staff of the armed forces. He was Hitler's first advisor on strategic and operational matters, and very much under his spell. His defence at his trial at Nuremberg was the classic that he had always been "subject to superior orders". He was hanged on 16 October 1946.*

On 8 May, what Stalin regarded as the main surrender was effected in Berlin. Present were Zhukov representing the Soviet Union; Air Chief Marshal Sir Arthur Tedder (Eisenhower's Deputy), General Carl Spaatz, USAAF, and General de Lattre de Tassigny, commanding the French First Army, representing the Western Allies. Into their presence strode Field Marshal Keitel, arrogantly saluting the Allied Delegation with his field marshal's baton. He was followed by General Hans-Jurgen Stumpff, commanding the Luftwaffe, his eyes full of impotent rage, and Friedeberg, grey with exhaustion and emotion. On being asked if he would sign, Keitel assented, shooting a malignant glance at Zhukov, his hand shaking. After the others had signed, the German delegation was dismissed.

By 10:43 p.m. Central European Time on 8 May the war against Germany was over. As the participants left, the Red Army guards outside joyfully fired their weapons into the air.

ABOVE At the Karlshorst, the Soviet Headquarters in Berlin, Marshal of the Soviet Union Georgi K Zhukov, Deputy Commander-in-Chief of the Soviet Forces signs the surrender terms.

BELOW The original Instrument of Surrender of German forces in Holland, north-west Germany and Denmark, signed by Field Marshal Montgomery and Admiral General von Friedeburg, among others, at 6.30 p.m. on 4 May.

Instrument of Surrender

of

All German armed forces in HOLLAND, in northwest Germany including all islands, and in DENMARK.

1. The German Command agrees to the surrender of all German armed forces in HOLLAND, in northwest GERMANY including the FRISIAN ISLANDS and HELIGOLAND and all other islands, in SCHLESWIG-HOLSTEIN, and in DENMARK, to the C.-in-C. 21 Army Group. This to include all naval ships in these areas. These forces to lay down their arms and to surrender unconditionally.

2. All hostilities on land, on sea, or in the air by German forces in the above areas to cease at 0800 hrs. British Double Summer Time on Saturday 5 May 1945.

3. The German command to carry out at once, and without argument or comment, all further orders that will be issued by the Allied Powers on any subject.

4. Disobedience of orders, or failure to comply with them, will be regarded as a breach of these surrender terms and will be dealt with by the Allied Powers in accordance with the accepted laws and usages of war.

5. This instrument of surrender is independent of, without prejudice to, and will be superseded by any general instrument of surrender imposed by or on behalf of the Allied Powers and applicable to Germany and the German armed forces as a whole.

6. This instrument of surrender is written in English and in German.

   The English version is the authentic text.

7. The decision of the Allied Powers will be final if any doubt or dispute arises as to the meaning or interpretation of the surrender terms.

B. L. Montgomery
Field-Marshal

4 May 1945
1830 hrs

RIGHT AND OPPOSITE Procedural document in English and German used by Canadian officers to obtain essential information from their Wehrmacht counterparts immediately following the unconditional surrender of Nazi Germany.

1

FIRST CANADIAN ARMY

SURRENDER PROFORMA 'B'

CAPITULATIONS-FORMULAR 'B'

____

(Name of unit, formation headquarterse etc)
(Name der Einheit, Abteilung, Befehlsstelle usw.)

____

(Name, eank and number of commanding officer)
(Name, Dienstgrad und Nummer des Befehlshabers)

Serial	NOTES	Nummer	Anmerkungen
1	You are required to give the information demanded overleaf accurateley in respect of the troops under your command and the area which you ocuppy.	1	Sie werden aufgefordert, genaue Angaben über die Ihnen unterstellten Truppen sowie das von Ihnen besetzte Gebiet zu geben.
2	This form and all the attached sheets with the exception of maps, must be fully completed in quadruplicate. All answers to questions must be typewritten or, if no typewritter is available, block lettering will be used.	2	Dieses Formular sowie alle beiliegenden Bogen, mit Ausnahme der Karten, müssen in 4 Exemplaren ausgefertigt werden. Alle Antworten müssen mit Schreibmaschine, oder falls nicht möglich, in Druckschrift geschrieben werden.
3	(a) Where maps are required only one copy of each map need be completed. (b) All information on the map will be indicated by a number. (c) A detailed statement will be attached to the map, numbered in the same way, a full description of the information required being given on the statement opposite the appropraite number.	3	(a) Falls Karten benötigt sind, wird jede Karte nur in einmaliger Ausführung beigelegt werden. (b) Einzelne Angaben auf der Karte werden nummeriert. (c) Eine Erklärung muß beigefügt werden, in welcher jede auf der Karte eingezeichnete Nummer genau erläutert wird.
4	As a guide to Allied Commanders this proforma should be returned by the German Commander responsible for its completion within the appropiate time limit shown below:- Unit commander — 6 hours Brigade (or equivalent) commander — 24 hours Division (or equivalent) commander — 48 hours Corps (or equivalent) commander — 72 hours	4	Folgende Fristen, binnen welcher der verantwortliche deutsche Befehlshaber das ausgefüllte Formular abzugeben hat, sind den alliierten Befehlshabern als Richtlinien gegeben:- Bataillons(Bzw. Abteilungs)-Kommandeur — 6 Std. Regiment(oder entsprechend Kommandeur) — 24 Std. Divisions(oder entsprechend Kommandeur) — 48 Std. Korps (oder entsprechend Kommandeur) — 72 Std.
-	Allied commanders in stating the time		Bei Festsetzung der Frist sind die

of return will however use their discretion where an extension is obviously justified.

5 The four copies of this form properly completed will be handed
to: Comd.147 Inf.Bde.
at: 19oo hours 8th May

6 You are warned that any failure to answer all questions correctly and completeley will be severely punished

<u>Serial</u> <u>Questions</u>

7,Attach a map showing the location of all flying bomb and rocket launching sites in your area.

8 Attach a map showing the following information concerning your area:

(a) Minefields(giving types of mines, exact locations and boundaries).
(b) Boobytrapped areas or buildings. Complete details will be furnished.
(c) Bridges, culverts, roads, buildings or any installation prepared for demolition.
(d) Routes open and usable by motor transport in your area.
(e) Routes open and usable by tanks in your area.

~~XXXXXXXXXXXXXXXXXXXXXXXXXXXXXXXXXXXXXXXXXXX~~

9 Attach a diagram showing the complete layout of your signal communications.

10 Attach a list of frequency and code signallotments giving full titles of headquarters and units in each case.

11 Attach nominal rolls of all officers in headquarters an units under your command.

<u>Note:</u> A nominal roll will be prepared in respect of each headquarters and unit showing the following information in respect of each officer.
(a) Rank, surname(in block letters) christian names,personal number(if any) and appointment.
(b) A note that the officer is a member of the German General Staff Corps (if applicable).
(c) Which officers, are, or have been, members of one or more of the following organisations:
GEHEIME FELDPOLIZEI NSKK

alliierten Befehlshaber ermächtigt dieselbe aus triftigen Gründen zu verlängern.

5 Die vier Exemplare dieses Fragebogens müssen nach genauer Ausfüllung abgegeben werden,
an: Comd.147 Inf.Brigade
in: 19oo hours 8th May

6 Sie sind gewarnt, daß ungenaue und unvollständige Beantwortungen der folgenden Fragen streng bestraft werden.

<u>Number</u> <u>FRAGEN</u>

7 Eine Karte beilegen mit Angabe über alle sich in Ihrem Bereich befindlichen V1 und V2 Abschußplätze.

8 Eine Karte mit folgenden Angaben beilegen über das von Ihnen besetzte Gebiet:
(a) Minenfelder (Arten der Minen,genaue geografische Lage sowie Grenzen der Minenfelder).
(b) Sprengfallen in Gebäuden und anderswo. Vollständige Einzelheiten müssen angegeben werden.
(c) Brücken,Übergänge,Straßen,Gebäude sowie andere Gegenstände die zur Sprengung vorbereitet sind.
(d) Straßen in Ihrem Gebiet, die frei u.fahrbar für Kraftfahrzeuge sind.
(e) Straßen in Ihrem Gebiet, die frei u.fahrbar für Panzerkampfwagen sind.

9 Eine Skizze beilegen mit genauen Angaben über Ihre Nachrichten-Verbindungen.

10 Alle Frequenzverteiler,Rufzeichentafel und Funkpläne sind beizufügen In jedem Falle voller Titel des Hauptquartiers und der unterstellten Einheiten geben.

11 Namenslisten beilegen aller Offiziere, die sich in den Ihnen unterstellten Stäben und Abteilungen befinden.

<u>Anmerkung:</u> Für jeden Stab und Einheit wird eine einzelne Namensliste der Offiziere angefertigt.

(a) Dienstgrad,Familienname(in Druckschrift) Vornamen,Nummer(falls zutreffend) und Stellung.
(b) Im Falle eines Generalstabsoffizieres muß dieses vermerkt werden.

(c) Welche Ihrer Offiziere sind oder waren Mitglieder folgender Organisationen:
GEHEIME FELDPOILZEI NSKK

BELOW Eisenhower's official farewell thank you note issued to the forces under his command in north-west Europe.

SUPREME HEADQUARTERS

ALLIED EXPEDITIONARY FORCE

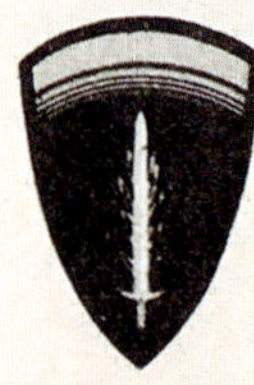

TO ALL MEMBERS OF THE ALLIED EXPEDITIONARY FORCE:

The task which we set ourselves is finished, and the time has come for me to relinquish Combined Command.

In the name of the United States and the British Commonwealth, from whom my authority is derived, I should like to convey to you the gratitude and admiration of our two nations for the manner in which you have responded to every demand that has been made upon you. At times, conditions have been hard and the tasks to be performed arduous. No praise is too high for the manner in which you have surmounted every obstacle.

I should like, also, to add my own personal word of thanks to each one of you for the part you have played, and the contribution you have made to our joint victory.

Now that you are about to pass to other spheres of activity, I say Good-bye to you and wish you Good Luck and God-Speed.

Dwight D. Eisenhower

RIGHT VE-Day edition of the Canadian Forces newspaper *The Maple Leaf*.

FOR CANADIAN FORCES IN ACTION

THE MAPLE LEAF EXTRA

WITH CANADIAN PRESS NEWS SERVICE

SPECIAL VICTORY EDITION

KAPUT

Page 2 THE MAPLE LEAF Wednesday, May 9, 1945

"CEASE FIRE" ORDER IN ALL EUROPE

Camera Records for History Signing of Surrender

War Ends in Five-Minute Flurry of Signatures As Nazi Surrender Completed

BY MAJ. J. D. MACFARLANE (Staff Writer, The Maple Leaf)

SHAEF (Paris)—The war in Europe is over. The Germans have accepted terms of complete and unconditional surrender of all land, sea and air forces simultaneously to the Allied Expeditionary Forces and the Russian High Command.

The surrender documents were signed at Allied Supreme Forward HQ in a schoolhouse in the French city of Rheims, at 0241 hours BDST, Monday, May 7, and the cease fire everywhere in Europe went into effect at 0001 hours today, Wednesday, May 9, 1945.

Churchill Gives Official Version

Blow-by-Blow Description In Final Round of Conflict

In Appreciation

Here is the Text of the Final Surrender Document Signed at Rheims by Nazi and Allied Officers

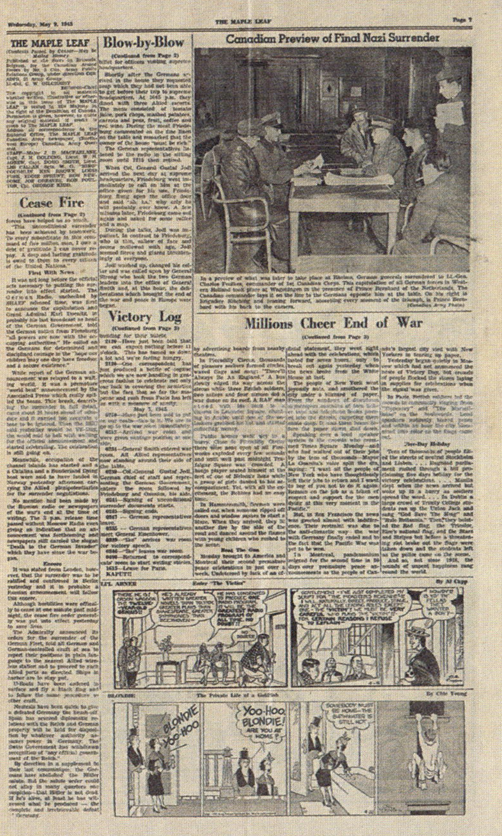

THE MAPLE LEAF

Blow-by-Blow

Canadian Preview of Final Nazi Surrender

Cease Fire

Victory Log

Millions Cheer End of War

VE-DAY CELEBRATIONS

TUESDAY 8 MAY 1945

On 8 May, great crowds waited in silence in London to hear Churchill announce from 10 Downing Street at 3.00 p.m., "The German War is at an end." They knew the war was over: that morning the *Daily Mirror's* strip cartoon character Jane had appeared completely naked, as she had always promised to do for peace. But at last it was official. People waved flags, sang, blew whistles, and massed in front of Buckingham Palace, shouting "We want the King." Soon he appeared on the balcony with his wife and daughters. They made eight such appearances before midnight. At one stage Churchill appeared with them. Bonfires, floodlights and searchlights lit up the capital, blacked out for nearly six years. Ships' sirens sounded the letter V in Morse.

New York exploded into a massive party. Office workers celebrated in the streets, and watched ticker tape and torn-up telephone

ABOVE Two WAAFs and an RAF pilot celebrate VE-Day in London. Non-uniform hats were very much the order of the day.

ABOVE Mrs Pat Burgess of Palmers Green hears the news that the war in Europe is over, and that her husband will soon be home.

SECOND WORLD WAR

CASUALTIES

SOVIET UNION: seven million in battle and seven million civilian casualties

POLAND: 20 per cent of pre-war population – nearly six million service and civilian casualties and deaths under occupation

FRANCE: 200,000 dead in battle and 400,000 from air raids or in concentration camps

BRITAIN AND COMMONWEALTH: suffered 344,000 armed service casualties and 60,000 civilian casualties by bombing

AMERICA: suffered 292,000 military casualties

GERMANY: four million servicemen and 600,000 civilians by air attack

ABOVE King George VI and Queen Elizabeth with Winston Churchill and Princess Elizabeth (left) and Princess Margaret (right) on the balcony of Buckingham Palace in London on 8 May 1945.

PRESIDENT HARRY S. TRUMAN *had been Vice-President for only 83 days when Roosevelt died. He had never been taken into Roosevelt's confidence on any of the important post-war issues America would face, and he knew nothing about the atomic bomb, but immediately authorised its production. The emerging problem was now Soviet expansionism. Truman accused the Russians of breaking the Yalta agreement over their treatment of Poland while expressing the hope that they would participate in the war against Japan.*

ABOVE American soldiers read *Stars and Stripes*, the first newspaper to hit the London streets announcing the German surrender. The paper was printed on the presses of *The Times* in London.

directories hurled from skyscrapers. St Patrick's Cathedral in New York was packed out with servicemen and women who covered their heads in handkerchiefs.

In Paris, the headlines in *Paris Soir* were six inches high. The citizens of this great city that had suffered so much stood on their balconies to watch a fly-past of Allied aircraft.

There was a footnote looming over these heartfelt celebrations, articulated by Churchill in his broadcast to the nation announcing victory over Germany, "but let us not forget that Japan with all her treachery and greed remains unsubdued." In Washington, President Truman warned his fellow countrymen that the war was only half won. British and American servicemen and women would certainly not forget it. They had friends and relatives fighting the Japanese in the Philippines, Okinawa, and Burma at that very moment.

The outcome of the North-West Europe campaign was not a foregone conclusion. The German Army, arguably the best in the world, despite suffering huge losses on the Eastern Front remained formidable to the end. Its morale was consistently high even when

ABOVE Ecstatic workers in New York's Wall Street clamber over the statue of George Washington as they celebrate war's end in Europe.

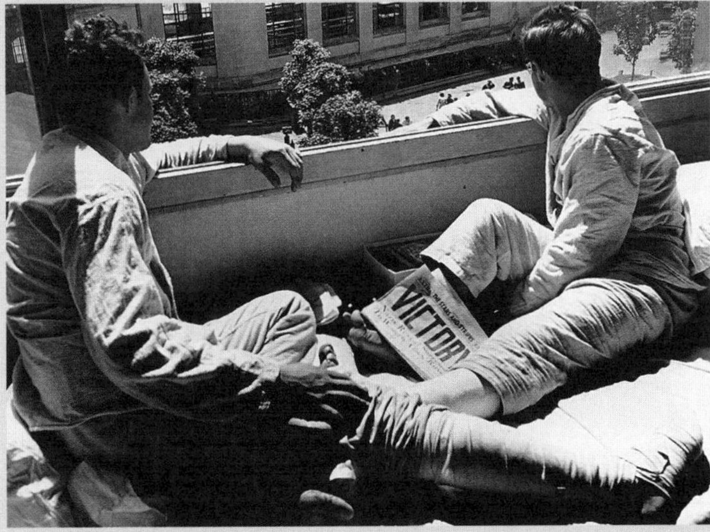

facing disaster. A brigadier who fought them in North Africa, Italy, and Arnhem remarked "however lightly the Germans were holding a position, the moment you threatened something they regarded as vital, their reaction would be swift and violent."

There were disagreements between the Allies, some bitter, but they were resolved. General Eisenhower takes the lion's share of the credit for maintaining Allied solidarity to the end.

Huge sacrifices were made by Allied soldiers, sailors and airmen in order to achieve Victory in Europe. Few of them were required to fight in the Far East because the war against Japan ended on 14 August 1945, just over three months after VE-Day.

TOP Crowds celebrate Victory in Europe in the Champs Elysées.

ABOVE LEFT Two wounded American soldiers, Private Al Stern of Brooklyn and Private Thorns Evans of Rahway, New Jersey watch crowds gathering in Paris to celebrate the news that Germany had surrendered.

ABOVE RIGHT British girls of the Picture Division of the London Office of War Information dance with American soldiers in Davies Street, London on 8 May 1945.

TRANSLATIONS

Page 46: Dutch Resistance report on German troop movements in and around Arnhem.
13 and 14 September 1944
ON both sides of the river IJssel, between Zwollen and Arnhem and in the Achterhoek they have made camp and they are still busy making camp:
SS. Division Hohenstaufen
Emblem on cars: *yellow* shield, *blue* rim, in which *blue* capital H and vertical *blue* sword.
Division staff probably in *Doetinchem*. No other details as yet. Other staffs, probably *regiment staffs*, in *Beekbergen* and *Epse*. *Beekbergen*: Ordn. Surv. Map 33. Zutphen W., publ. '34,
a. 13.65-63.95: Hotel.
Signs: IIV A.R. Halt.Abt.IIa and IIbn.
b. 14,1 – 63,7: Abt IVb Skalke Jager.
c. 14,3 – 63,87 : Post Office, *Red* flag with *white* F.
d. 14,25 – 63,9 : *Red* flag with *white* flash of lightning.
Further I/20; VI; SS Jense and another 4 units.
Total number in Beekbergen: approx. 300 SS men. *White* and *red*.
Epse: Cafe "De Pessink" (fork in road Deventer-Zutphen, Deventer-Lochem): Red flag with white F. approx. 100 SS red.
Deventer: approx. 50 SS white.
Diepenveen: approx. 500 SS white. Saw: 3 armoured vehicles, length 4.5 m, height 1.50 m., armoured with heavy m.g. or PaK (anti-tank gun).
Saw: 8 piece PaK (6 cm)
Gorssel: approx. 250 SS red.
Road Apeldoorn-Zutphen between De Kar and Empe.
approx. 300 SS red, saw: 6 piece psK (3.7 cm)
Signs Grau: grau 2 and grau 3.
Klarenbeek: Hotel: Abt. IVa and Flak 10 Schraubs approx. 10 SS white.
Loenen: Hotel Eikenboom: approx. 150 SS white and red. Sign [red]
Vaassen: approximately 50 SS white.
Apeldoorn: approximately 100 SS white (Hohenstaufen)
Signs I/19 and II/19 (furthermore old SS occupations. 100 men).
Direction Hoenderlo: approx. 80 SS
Arnhem: Meldekopf Hohenstaufen.
H.V.P. Hohenstaufen.
Sax_and_Weimarkazerne (barracks). Signs M O; H i; saw car SS with [pink]
Probably taken on in association with Hohenstaufen: approx. 100 W.H. pink with 1 tank (6 cm. canon) and 20 light armoured vehicles.
Next: [4 and whiter – pink]
In Arnhem, Velp and Ooseterbeek: approx. 1500 SS (yellow, pink, white and red).
Achterhoek: SS in Vorden and Doetinchem)Div. Stab?!!!).
Estimate of the total seen: approx. 3500–4000 SS men Hohenstafen.

Further notices:
Arnhem, 14 September: Willemskazern: O.K.W. Feldjager. [eagle]
Total of 400–500 men W.H. white and light green.
In addition: Fliegerfeld division.
saw car W.L. [green]
Oosterbeek-Wolfheze 14 Sept. approx. 750 WH. red, approx. 30 pieces 10 cm filed.
EPSE 13 September: 2500 barrels with 200 L. of petrol still there. [red]
Apeldoorn 13 September:
Airforce: Willem III barracks: Listening equipment is removed.
Current occupation:
A.F. 25 W.L. brown; 50 W.L. red (e.g. O.K.W. Panzerjager)
Army 100 WH blue
100 Grune Pol.
Defence: Emplacement 4 piece quad flak 2 cm.
Zutphen 13 September.

Page 66: A letter home by a Wehrmacht soldier of the 212th Volksgrenadier Division during the German advance at the Battle of the Bulge.

Luxemburg, 21.12.44
Dear Aunty Paula!
Three days before Christmas! And we are advancing. Until today, I didn't have any Christmas feeling! Only today did we have the first snow. I think that you would have had a very poor Christmas with us here. Because the Americans leave quite nice and pretty things here. Just have a look at this writing paper! You have no idea what else there is. Millions of pencils, thousands of socks and stockings, wines and liquers, jams, preserved fruits, sugar. In a word, abundance of all kind of things! One has to see something like this, otherwise you wouldn't believe it. Everything is lying around in the shops on the floor and the peasants are stepping in it with their dirty boots and digging into it.
Have you received the 100RM, yet?! –
Consider it a Christmas present from me,
Kind regards,
Korli

Page 110: Letter by General Leclerc, commanding the French 2nd Armoured Division, to his wife.

German Army
Command Strasbourg
Blauwolkengasse 25 (Tel: 20084)
The Commandant
Strasbourg, 24/11/44
My darling,
Yesterday evening at 4.00 p.m. the French flag was hoisted above the spire of Strasbourg cathedral! An unforgettable day after five extraordinary days of battle. Once again, Provicence really led me by the hand.
Our men were magnificent. Some wonderful officers fell, including de la Horrie (Iris' suitor) who had just taken control of Badonviller. The children are well.
Henri was in the thick of the fighting.
I kiss you very hard
Leclerc

Page 111: French propaganda leaflet. This was fired in a propaganda shell by the French collaborators on Free French Forces fighting with the Americans in the Vosges region of south-east France in November 1944.
[front]
The surprise of the party
[back]
FEELING AT HOME
An American war correspondent cables New York with the following details about the life led by American soldiers in Paris.
Once or twice a week, the soldiers are taken to a performance in a nightclub or a dance hall.
Naturally, soldiers sometimes want to have a party. But an evening without women is not much fun. The problem is solved by telephoning the Committee and asking for 20 or 30 young girls. They are fetched by car and, naturally, they are taken home again by car. The evening is livened up as a result.
An Allied soldier can choose a companion for the whole of his stay in Paris. Here again, the Committee works in liaison with the unit. The young girl must belong to the same social class as the soldier. Furthermore, it can be said without fear of contradiction that the young girls come from the best families in Paris. Thanks to this function of the Committee, the Allied soldier feels at home in Paris and doesn't suffer so much from being separated from his family.
The Americans are having fun...
But what do the serving soldiers who are engaged to these female companions think about it?

Pages 139: Hitler's Political Testament dictated by the Führer to his secretary Frau Junge and signed at 4.00 a.m. on 29 April in the Reich Chancellary bunker.
MY POLITICAL TESTAMENT
Since 1914 when, as a volunteer, I made my modest contribution in the world war which was forced upon the Reich, over 30 years have now passed.
In these three decades only love for my people and loyalty to my people have guided me in all my thoughts, actions and life. They give me the strength to make the gravest decisions such as have never before been demanded of any

mortal. I have exhausted all my time, my energy and my health in these three decades. It is untrue that I or anybody else in Germany wanted war in 1939. It was desired and instigated exclusively by those international statesmen who were either of Jewish origin or working for Jewish interests. I have made too many proposals for the limitation and control of armaments, which posterity will not be able to deny for all eternity, for the responsibility for the outbreak of this war to be placed on me. Further, I have never desired that after the first, tragic, world war there should be a second one against England, let alone America. Centuries will pass but from the ruins of our towns and monuments of art, hatred for the people ultimately responsible will always grow anew, the people whom we have to thank for all this: international Jewry and its helpers.
As late as three days before the outbreak of the German–Polish war I suggested to the British Ambassador in Berlin a solution of the German problem similar to the one in the case of the Saar district under international control. This offer, too, cannot be denied. It was only rejected because those with decisive influence in British politics wanted the war, partly in the expectation of business advantages, partly under the influence of propanganda organized by International Jewry.
I also made it quite plain that if once again the peoples of Europe were to be regarded merely as share-holdings of the international conspirators of money and finance, then the people that bear the real guilt for the murderous struggle would also have to answer for it: Jewry! I also left no-one in doubt that this time must not happen that millions of children of Europeans of the Aryan nations would die of hunger,that millions of grown men would meet their death, and hundreds of thousands of women and children be burned amd bombed to death in towns, without the real culprit being made to pay for his guilt even if in a more humane way.
After six years "struggle" which in spite of all setbacks will one day go down in history as the most glorious and courageous manifestation of a nation's will to live, I cannot leave the city which is the capital of this country. As our forces are too small to make any further stand against the enemy attack at this place and the value of personal resistance is being gradually diminshed by misguided and unprincipled creatures, I wish, by staying in this town, to join my fate with millions of others have also taken upon themselves. Besides, I do not want to fall into the hands of enemies who for the entertainment of their masses fed with hate propaganda, require a new spectacle organized by Jews.
I had therefore decided to remain in Berlin, and there to choose voluntary death at the moment when I believed that the seat of office of the Führer and Chancellor at once can no longer be defended. I die with a joyful heart in the awareness of the immeasurable deeds and achievements of our soldiers at the Front, of our women at home, the achievements of our peasants and workers, and of the contribution, unique in history, of our youth that bears my name.
It goes without saying that I thank you from the bottom of my heart, and it is my with that despite everything they should not give up the struggle under any circumstances, but continue it against the enemies of the Fatherland, wherever they may be, true to the principles of the great Clausewitz. From the sacrifice of our soldiers and from my own comradeship with them unto death, there will one day, in one way or another the seeds will grow in German history of a glorious renaissance of the National Socialist movement and thus the realization of the true national community.
Many very brave men and women have resolved to link their lives with mine to the last. I have asked, and finally ordered, them not to do this but to take part in the continuing struggle of the nation. I ask the commanders of the Armies, the Navy and the Air Force to strengthen by all possible means the spirit of resistance of our soldiers in the spirit of National Socialism, with special emphasis on the fact that I myself as the founder of this movement, have also preferred death to a cowardly flight or, worse still, capitulation.
May it one day be a part of the code of honour of the German officer, as it is already the case in our Navy, that the surrender of a district or town is unthinkable and that above all leaders must in this set a shining example of faithful devotion to duty until death.
Before my death I expel the former Reich Marshal Hermann Goering from the party and deprive him of all rights which he may enjoy by virtue of the decree of June 29th 1941, and also by virtue of my statement in the Reichstag on September 1st 1939. I appoint in his place Grand Admiral Doenitz as President of the Reich and Supreme Commander of the Armed Forces.
Before my death I expel the former Reich Leader SS and Minister of the Interior, Heimlich Himmler, from the party and from all offices of State. In his place I appoint Gauleiter Karl Hanke as Reich Leader SS and Chief of the German Police, and Gauleiter Paul Giesler as Reich Minister of the Interior.
Goering and Himmler have done immeasurable harm to the country and the whole nation by secretly negotiating with the enemy without my knowledge and against my will, and by illegally attempting to seize power in the State for themselves, not to speak of their disoyalty to my person. In order to give the German people a government composed of honourable men, a government which will fulfill its duty to continue the war with all available means, I appoint as leaders of the nation the following members of the new Cabinet:
President of the Reich: Doenitz
Party Minister: Bormann
Foreign Minister: Seyss-Inquart
Minister of Interior: Gauleiter Giesler
Minister for War: Doenitz
C-in-C of the Army: Schoerner
C-in-C of Navy: Doenitz
C-in-C of the Air Force: Greim
Reich Leader SS and Chief of the German Police: Gauleiter Hanke
Economics: Funk
Agriculture: Backe
Justice: Thierack
Education and Public Worship: Dr Scheel
Propaganda: Dr Naumann
Finance: Schwerin-Crossigk
Labour: Dr Hupfauer
Munitions: Saur
Leader of the German Labour Front and Member of the Reich Cabinet: Reich Minister Dr Ley

Although a number of these men, such as Martin Bormann, Dr Goebbels etc, together with their wives, have joined me of their own free will and did not wish to leave the capital of the Reich under any circumstances, but were willing to perish with me here, I must nevertheless ask them to obey my request, and in the present case, set the interests of the nation above their own feelings. By their work and loyalty they will after my death be just as close to be as comrades as I hope that my spirit will remain amongst them and always go with them. Let them be hard, but never unjust; above all let them never fear to counsel their actions, and esteem the honour of the nation above everything else in the world. Finally, let them by conscious of the fact that our task of building a National Socialist state constitutes the work of the coming centuries and that this places every single person under an obligation always to serve the common interest and to subordinate his own advantage to it. Of all Germans, all National Socialists, men, women and all soldiers of the Armed Forces I demand that they be faithful and obedient unto death to the new government and their President.
Above all I charge the leaders of the nation and those under them to scrupulous observance of the racial laws and to merciless opposition to the universal poisoner of all peoples, international Jewry.
BERLIN, 29 April 1945 4.00 hrs. Adolf Hitler
Witnesses: Dr Josef Goebbels, Wilhelm Buergdorf, Martin Bormann, Hans Krebs.

Page 139: One of the last secret telegrams sent by Hitler from the Reich Chancellary bunker.
Telegraph office: 13 LBMR: 0476
Date: 30.4.45 At: 03.10 hourse
CONFIDENTIAL
Telegram +FRR MBBS 06274 29.4 22.30
FRR LDN WISMAR.=
After receiving commando documents must be treated as confidential
Stabsobermeister (colonel general) Goere.
The following transmission must be forwarded immediately to the Wehrmacht authority field office north. According to the communication. Army authority moved west from Rheinsberg towards Weismar. A part of WFST should already be there – radio telegraph should be forwarded immediately to the relevant office in charge: radio message from Grau 2 A decoded:
"frr Gen Colonel Jodl Zeppelin)
The following must be reported to me immediately:
1) Where are the advances from "Wenck"??
2) When will they further attack?
3) Where is the 9th Army?
4) In what direction is the 9th Army breaking through?
5) Where is the advance front of the "Hoste"?
Adolf Hitler
Answer immediately to the mar. news. department of the marine war leadership via radio through army radio station Ploen, telegraph via marine MSBN marine –MBBS – MWHB) to Ploen.=
MNA / SKL +s

INDEX

Page numbers in *italics* refer to images and captions.

CREDITS

The publishers would like to thank the following for their valuable assistance with the preparation of this book:

Imperial War Museum
Tony Richards (Department of Documents); Alan Jeffreys (Department of Exhibits and Firearms); Andrew McDonnell and Paul Bailey (Department of Exhibitions); Christopher Hunt (Department of Printed Books); Terry Charman (Department of Research and Information); Jeremy Richards, Glyn Biesty, David Parry, Ian Carter, Chris Plant, Alan Wakefield and Emma Crocker (Photograph Archive); Angela Godwin, Dr Christopher Dowling, Elizabeth Bowers and Gemma Maclagan (Public Services Division); Margaret Brooks and John Stopford-Pickering (Sound Archive).

Airborne Museum "Hartenstein": Robert Sigmond and Adrian Groeneweg OBE
Bastogne Historical Center: Madame Véronique Huet
Deborah Cooney (US National Archives research)
La Coupole, Saint-Omer: Monsieur Le Maner
Friends of the 385th Bomb Group and Memorial Museum: Roger Feller
Jane Gregory
Barbara Levy
Jack and Bridget Livesey
Musée de la Bataille des Ardennes à la Roche-en-Ardennes: Monsieur Bouillon
Musée Mémorial des Combats de la Poche de Colmar: Christian Burgert, Jean-Marc Weckner and Lionel Charluteau
Musée Maison Mathelin à Bastogne: Monsieur Cockaerts
Musée National d'Histoire Militaire Diekirch: Roland Gaul
Nationaal Bevrijdingsmuseum 1944-1945: Wiel P.H. Lenders et Frank van den Bergh
Nationaal Oorlogs- en Verzetsmuseum: P.J.J. Klassen
Musée Pierre-Noël: Daniel Grandidier, Jean-Claude Fombaron and Madame Garnier
Jean Restayn
Peter Steinkamp

Specially commissioned maps
©Welbeck Books Limited 2005
Editorial research and checking: Jack Livesay
Design: Mary Ferdinand and Martin Brown

Artwork
© Jean Restayn

Picture Credits
The majority of photographs reproduced in this book have been taken from the collections of the Photograph Archive at the Imperial War Museum. The reference numbers for each of the photographs are listed below, giving the page number, location and reference number.

Key: t = top, b = bottom, c = centre, l = left & r = right

2-3 FRA 101879, 4 BU 3419, 8 t EA 25491, 8 c B5218, 9 t H39070, 9 tr TR 1042, 14 t HU 82258, 14 b KY32662, 15 t OWIL 32400, 15 bl OWIL36141, 16 t EA 35245, 16 b B 8463, 18 IA 33992, 19 EA t 33702, 19 b NA 20780, 21 t IAP 34055, 21 b FRA 200968, 21 bl NYF 37995, 21 br EA 37765, 24 GER 1370W, 25 t CH 13428, 25 c CH16281, 25 b HU 91464, 28 HU 81701, 29 tl COR U673389ACME, 29 tr BU 481A, 29 bl BU 862, 29 br BU 483, 30 tl B 7407, 30 NA tr 8923, 30 b PL 37529, 32 t K 7590, 32 b EA 37750, 33 t K 7588, 33 c H 38770, 35 t CL 1173, 35 bl EA 39841, 35 br CL 1234, 38 b B 10173, 39 t B 10175, 39 b BU 1062, 40 tl BU 2411, 40 b B10294, 42 t BU 1108, 42 br BU 1098, 43 MH 2061, 44 t IL 40971, 44 c BU 1115, 44 r HU 2131, 48 C 4668, 49 t HU 82259, 49 b HU 63664, 50 t A 26233, 50 bl A 26269, 50 br MO151051, 52 EA 37951, 53 c EA 41420, 56 l EA 44314, 56 r EA 44330, 57 t EA 36896, 58 tl EA 44315, 58 tr EA 42938, 58 bl HU 82263, 58 br PL 43803, 62 EA 48001, 63 t FA 47965, 63 b EA 48015, 65 tl EA 47962, 65 bl HN 46178, 65 br EA 68789, 68 t ULT 399087, 68 b EA 49928, 69 EA 47958, 70 b EA 48296, 71 r EA50367, 77 b EA 48892, 78 t FRA 101879, 80 NAM 203, 81 NAP 275888, 82 NAM 234, 84 B 14413, 85 t B 14608, 85 b HU 82277, 85 c AP 7384F, 87 tl KY 55480, 87 tr AP 59610, 87 b KY 54468, 90 S & G 56776, 91 EA 56522, 92 tr KY 56697, 92 b EA 56685, 95 t BU 2154, 95 b BU 2504, 96 t BU 2143, 96 b KY 488980, 98 l BU 2313, 98 b FOX 60432, 100 Department of Documents, 102 KA 276829, 103 tl MH 12850, 103 tr EA 60105, 103 b KY 60438, 105 t MOI 68189, 105 bl EA 61390, 105 br EA 63145, 106 EA 44924, 107 tl EA 44782, 107 tr EA 44922, 107 b MISC 46871, 108 tr NA 673, 108 c KY 59437, 108 b KY 488320, 115 tr EA 36158, 115 bl AD 276105, 116tl HU 4052, 116 c HU 44931, 116 b EA 13271, 118-119 Department of Documents, 122 BU 3635m 123 tl BU 4475, 123 tr BU 3419, 123 b BU 5076, 125 t HU 82280, 125 br BU 4355, 127 FRA 105752, 128 t EA 65160, 128 bl EA 62972, 128 br BU 3821, 129 BU 4030, 130 l BU 3812, 130 r BU 4025, 131 Department of Documents, 132 r EA 62455, 133 tr KY 64230, 133 bl EA 64834, 134 tl EA 6617, 134 bl KY 66733, 137 NYP 62569, 139 t Department of Documents, 140 l BU 3541, 140 r BU 5230, 141 t BU 5705, 141 br BU 7587, 142 tl BU 6051, 142 tr BU 5354, 142 b BU 5360, 144 BU 5210, 145 l BU 5157, 145 r FRA 203386, 145 b KY 66972, 146 tl EA 65715, 146 tr FRA 203288, 146 br FRA 203382, 146 cl AP 69125, 151 Department of Documents, 152 l HN 91225, 152 r FOX 66398, 153 l NYP 64417, 153 tr MH 21835, 153 br EA 65943, 155 t KY 66850, 155 l FRA 203355, 155 r FA 65796

Photographs from sources from outside the Imperial War Museum:

Airbourne Museum 'Hartenstein', Utrechtseweg 232, 6862 AZ Osterbeek, Netherlands: 36, 37, 46, 47; /Bastonge Historical Center, Colline du Mardasson, B-6600 Bastogne, Belgium: 72, 73, 150; /Bundesarchiv-Militarchiv, Wiesentalstrase 10, 79115 Feriburg, Germany: 139 b
Canadiansoldiers.com: 125 bl; /Dwight D. Eisenhower Library, Abilene, Kansas: 11; /Jean-Claude Fombaron: 22-23, 111; /Friends of the 385th Bomb Group and Memorial Museum, rue de l'eglise, Perlé, Luxembourg: 117, 120, 121; /Getty Images: Bettmann 40 t, 53 b, 57 b, 137tl, 138tr, 154, /Robert Capa/Keystone 98 tr; /Hulton Archive 108 tl; /Hulton-Deutsch Collection/CORBIS/Corbis 145 t; /Keystone-France/Gamma-Rapho 77, 93 r; /Leonard McCombe/Picture Post/Hulton Archive 114; /Photo 12/UIG 15 b; /Library of Congress: 93 l; /Universal History Archive/Universal Images Group 137 tr; /Meteorlogical Office (UK): 12, 13; /Musée Mémorial des Combat de la Poche de Colmar, 25 rue du Conseil: 67, 110; /Musée National d'Historie Militaire Diekirch, 10 Bamertal, L-9209 Diekirch, Luxembourg: 55, 66, 75, 75; /The Museum of Danish Resistance 1940-1945: 143; /National Archives and Records Administration, Washington 8 b, 9 br, 53 t, 61, 65 tr, 70 tl, 70 tr, 71 tl , 71 cl, 78 b, 90 t, 96 tr, 133 tl, 134tr; /NZ Bomber Command Association archives, Dick Broadbent collection: 115tl; /Nationaal Bevrijdingsmuseum 1944-45 Wylerbaan 4, Groesbeek, Netherlands: 88, 89, 101; */Nationaal Oorlogs-en Verzetmuseum, Museumpark 1, 5825 AM, Overloon, Netherlands: 148-149; /Papers of The Rt Hon Viscount Montgomery of Alamein CMG CBE and the Imperial War Museum, Department of Documents: 60, 147;* /Photo12/Coll-DITE/USIS 92 tl
The Pierre-Noel Museum, Museum of Life in the Upper Vosges, place George Trimouille, 88107 St-Die-des-Vosges, France: 112, 113; /Public Domain: 27b, 42 bl, 107 r; /Topfoto: 39 bl, 132 l; /Ullstein Bild 138 tl; /Voller Ernst/Evgenij Chaldej: 138b

Every effort has been made to acknowledge correctly and contact the source and/or copyright holder of each picture and Welbeck Publishing apologises for any unintentional errors or omissions, which will be corrected in future editions of this book.

21.
Montgomery
1. Gen. Bradley
2. Gen. Anderson
V., VII., VIII., XIX.
1., 2., 4., 9., 29., 30., 79., 90. J.D.
2., 3., Pz.Div.
82., 101., L.L.
6., 70., Pz.Brig.
5. R.Btl.
I., VIII., XII., XXX.
3.Kan. 3., 15., 43., 49., 50., 51., 76. J.D.
7., 9., 11. Pz.Div.
6. L.L.
56, 71, 185, 227. Jnf.Brig.
2.kan., 4., 8., 27., 33., 41. Pz.Brig.
1., 4. S.S.
331. J.D.
326. J.D.
49.
85. J.D.
348.
116. Pz.
6. F.S.
621 (ost)
Schrader
245.
84 J.D.
17. Lw.
89.
LXXXI.
711. (bo.)
346. (bo.)
LXXXVI.
LXXXIV.
II. F.S.
XXXXVII. Pz.
Pz. Gr. West
7.
Tr. Üb. Pl. Camp de Avours
B
LXV.
CHERBOURG
LE HAVRE
ROUEN
PORTSMOUTH
BRIGHTON
HASTINGS
EASTBOURNE
Insel Wight
CALAIS
BOULOGNE
Abbeville
Dieppe
Fécamp
Bayeux
CAEN
Lisieux
Falaise
Flers
Argentan
Alençon
Avranches
Granville
Fougères
Mayenne
Laval
LE MANS
Chartres
Evreux
Vernon
Mantes
Pontoise
VERSAILLES
Dreux
Elbeuf
Der Kanal